Air War D-Day

Volume 3

Winged Pegasus and The Rangers

Other volumes in this series

Air War D-Day Winged Pegasus and The Rangers

Air War D-Day

Volume 3

Winged Pegasus and
The Rangers

Martin W. Bowman

Pen & Sword
AVIATION

First Published in Great Britain in 2013 by
Pen & Sword Aviation
an imprint of
Pen & Sword Books Ltd
47 Church Street, Barnsley, South Yorkshire S70 2AS

A CIP catalogue record for this book is
available from the British Library.

Typeset in 10/12pt Palatino
by GMS Enterprises

Printed and bound in England by
CPI Group (UK) Ltd, Croydon, CR0 4YY

Pen & Sword Books Ltd incorporates the Imprints of Pen & Sword
Aviation, Pen & Sword Family History, Pen & Sword Maritime, Pen & Sword
Military, Pen & Sword Discovery, Wharncliffe Local History, Wharncliffe
True Crime, Wharncliffe Transport, Pen & Sword Select, Pen & Sword
Military Classics, Leo Cooper, The Praetorian Press, Remember When,
Seaforth Publishing and Frontline Publishing.

For a complete list of Pen & Sword titles please contact
PEN & SWORD BOOKS LIMITED

47 Church Street, Barnsley, South Yorkshire, S70 2AS, England
E-mail: enquiries@pen-and-sword.co.uk
Website: www.pen-and-sword.co.uk

Contents

Air War D-Day - Winged Pegasus and The Rangers

Acknowledgements

I am enormously grateful to the following people for their time and effort and kind loan of photos etc, not least to my fellow author and friend Graham Simons, for getting this to press-ready standard and for his detailed work on maps and photographs: My thanks to Ray Alm; Ed 'Cotton' Appleman; James Roland Argo; Peter Arnold; John Avis; Les Barber; Harry Barker; Mike Bailey; Carter Barber; Neil Barber, author of *The Day The Devils Dropped In*; E. W. D. Beeton; Franklin L. Betz; Bill Bidmead; Rusty Bloxom, Historian, Battleship Texas; Lucille Hoback Boggess; Prudent Boiux; August C. Bolino; Dennis Bowen; Tom Bradley; Eric Broadhead; Stan Bruce; K. D. Budgen; Kazik Budzik KW VM; Les Bulmer; Reginald 'Punch' Burge; Donald Burgett; Chaplain Burkhalter; Lol Buxton; Jan Caesar; R. H. 'Chad' Chadwick; Noel Chaffey; Mrs J. Charlesworth; Chris Clancy; Roy Clark RNVR; Ian 'Nobby' Clark; P. Clough; Johnny Cook DFM; Malcolm Cook; Flight Lieutenant Tony Cooper; Lieutenant-Colonel Eric A. Cooper-Key MC; Cyril Crain; Mike Crooks; Jack Culshaw, Editor, *The Kedge Hook*; Bill Davey; S. Davies; Brenda French, Dawlish Museum Society; John de S. Winser; Abel L. Dolim; Geoffrey Duncan; Sam Earl; *Eighth Air Force News; Eastern Daily Press*; Chris Ellis; Les 'Tubby' Edwards; W. Evans; Frank R. Feduik; Ron Field; Wolfgang Fischer; Robert Fitzgerald; Eugene Fletcher; Captain Dan Flunder; John Foreman; Wilf Fortune; H. Foster; Lieutenant-Commander R. D. Franks DSO; Jim Gadd; Leo Gariepy; Patricia Gent; Lieutenant Commander Joseph H. Gibbons USNR; Larry Goldstein; Bill Goodwin; Franz Goekel; Lieutenant Denis J. M. Glover DSC RNZNVR; John Gough; Peter H. Gould; George 'Jimmy' Green RNVR; Albert Gregory; Nevil Griffin; Edgar Gurney BEM; R. S. Haig-Brown; Leo Hall, Parachute Regt Assoc.; Günter Halm; Roland 'Ginger' A. Hammersley DFM; Madelaine Hardy; Allan Healy; Andre Heintz; Basil Heaton; Mike Henry DFC, author of *Air Gunner*; Vic Hester; Reverend R. M. Hickey MC; Lenny Hickman; Elizabeth Hillmann; Bill Holden; Mary Hoskins; Ena Howes; Pierre Huet; J. A. C. Hugill; Antonia Hunt; Ben C. Isgrig; Jean Irvine; Orv Iverson; George Jackson; Major R. J. L. Jackson; Robert A. Jacobs; G. E. Jacques; Marjorie Jefferson; Bernard M. Job RAFVR; Wing Commander 'Johnnie' Johnson DSO* DFC*; Percy 'Shock' Kendrick MM; the late Jack Krause; Cyril Larkin; Reg Lilley; John Lincoln, author of *Thank God and the Infantry*; Lieutenant Brian Lingwood RNVR; Wing Commander A. H. D. Livock; Leonard Lomell; P. McElhinney; Ken McFarlane; Don McKeage; Hugh R. McLaren; John McLaughlin; Nigel McTeer: Ron Mailey; Sara Marcum; Ronald Major; Walt Marshall; Rudolph May; Ken Mayo; Alban Meccia; Claude V. Meconis; Leon E. Mendel; Harold Merritt; Bill Millin for kindly allowing me to quote from his book, *Invasion;* Bill Mills; John Milton; Alan Mower; Captain Douglas Munroe; *A Corpsman Remembers D-Day Navy Medicine 85,* No.3 (May-June 1994); Major Tom Normanton; General Gordon E. Ockenden; Raymond Paris; Bill Parker, National Newsletter Editor, Normandy Veterans; Simon Parry; Albert Pattison; Helen Pavlovsky; Charles Pearson; Eric 'Phil' Phillips DFC MiD; T. Platt; Franz Rachmann; Robert J. Rankin; Lee Ratel; Percy Reeve; Jean Lancaster-Rennie; Wilbur Richardson; Helmut Romer; George Rosie; The Royal Norfolk Regiment; Ken Russell; A. W. Sadler; Charles Santarsiero; Erwin Sauer; Frank Scott; Ronald Scott; Jerry Scutts; Major Peter Selerie; Alfred Sewell; Bob Shaffer; Reg Shickle; John R. Slaughter; Ben Smith Jr.; *SOLDIER Magazine; Southampton Southern Evening Echo;* Southwick House, HMS *Dryad*, Southwick, Portsmouth; Bill Stafford; Allen W. Stephens; Roy Stevens; Mrs E. Stewart; Henry Tarcza; Henry 'Buck' Taylor; June Telford; E. J. Thompson; Charles Thornton; Robert P. Tibor; Dennis Till; Edward J. Toth; Walt Truax; Jim Tuffell; Russ Tyson; US Combat Art Collection, Navy Yard, Washington DC; Thomas Valence; John Walker; Herbert Walther; Ed Wanner; R. H. G. Weighill; Andrew Whitmarsh, Portsmouth Museum Service; 'Slim' Wileman; Jim Wilkins; E. G. G. Williams; Deryk Wills, author of *Put On Your Boots and Parachutes! The US 82nd Airborne Division;* Jack Woods; Len Woods; Waverly Woodson.

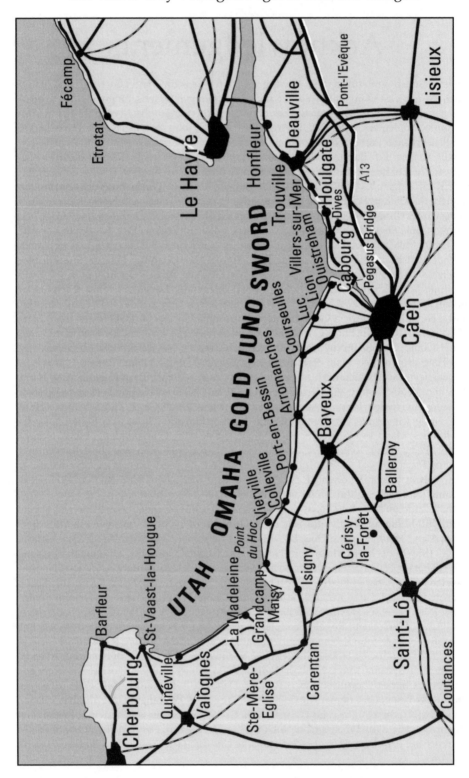

Chapter 1

Hold Until Relieved

'Citizens of France! I am proud to have again under my command the gallant forces of France. Fighting beside their allies, they will play a worthy part in the liberation of their homeland. Because the initial landing has been made on the soil of your country, I repeat my message to the peoples of other occupied countries in Western Europe. Follow the instructions of your leaders. A premature uprising of all Frenchmen may prevent you from being of maximum help to your country in the critical hour. Be patient. Prepare.
General Dwight D. Eisenhower Broadcast to France, June 6.

'The fighting ebbed away. It had now become clear that with the available forces alone, a success here could no longer be achieved. The British paratroops were not going to let themselves be overthrown so easily. The lack of success was a shock. We had not expected something like this. It had always been predicted that we would throw an attacker back into the sea at once.'

21st Panzer Division history. Parts of the 125th Panzer-Grenadier Regiment tried to dislodge the 12th British Parachute Battalion in a thrust toward Ranville with artillery support. On the other side of the Orne, elements of the 192nd Panzer-Grenadier Regiment failed in their counter-attacks to dislodge the 7th Parachute Battalion at Benouville and Le Port but were beaten off with heavy losses. Denied the support of the 12th SS Panzer, 21st Panzer was instructed to break off its attack, re-cross the Orne using the one surviving bridge over the river at Caen and drive towards 'Sword' Beach. But half 21st Panzer's infantry and part of the reconnaissance and assault-gun battalions were battling with 6th Airborne; so 21st Panzer could divert only its main tank strength (two tank battalions of Panzer-Regiment 22) westward.

The numbers of Panzer tanks that finally reached the invasion area could be numbered on the fingers of one hand. Had more Panzers reached the British and Canadian beaches sooner, the enterprise could have resulted in disaster for the Allies. As it was, 21st Panzer were stopped in their tracks.

While the bridges across the Caen Canal and the Orne were being successfully secured and held, the remainder of the 5th Parachute Brigade group were about their other tasks. The 12th and 13th Parachute Battalions had been detailed to seize the village of Le Bas de Ranville and the Ranville-le-Mariquet areas. To do so would be to establish a firm base east of the river and the canal and thus provide a starting point for subsequent operations. The 12th Battalion dropped at about 1 am on 6 June and were widely scattered, for the wind was still high. Soon after landing, small parties of men began to dribble into the rendezvous, a quarry near the dropping zone. By 11 am the battalion was taking up a line of defence round the village of Le Bas de Ranville, which was in their hands by 4 pm. An hour later the Germans launched a heavy counter-attack supported by tanks, armoured fighting vehicles and self-propelled guns. A hedge on the right of the battalion's position was held by Lieutenant John Sim MC and twelve men, who allowed the Germans to come very close. Resisting the temptation to open fire on the clanking enemy guns, they engaged instead the infantry behind them, killed some twenty of them and then, having lost all but four of their number, withdrew a short distance, after holding the position for a very important hour and a half during which the rest of the defence was organized. Elsewhere, along the perimeter, after close and determined fighting, during which an enemy tank was destroyed by a gammon bomb, the Germans were beaten back.

Captain John Sim, 12th Battalion, Parachute Regiment:
'Finally, the evening came - the evening of 5 June, when we got into our lorries and were transported to the airfield. We collected our chutes and the lorries took us around the perimeter, miles away into the country where our aircraft had been dispersed. The aircraft that we, the battalion, were going to jump out of was the Stirling, which had been coughed up by Bomber Command for us to use. We were right out in the countryside, a peaceful June evening, lovely and calm.

'We just sat and talked for a while amongst ourselves and then the padre came whipping up in his jeep and we had a little prayer. He wished us well and then he dashed off again to another aircraft. Then came the jeep of the RAF crew roaring up and they got out and said, 'All right you chaps. Don't worry! Piece of cake! We'll get you there! It was a tremendous, exciting, light-hearted atmosphere.

'We emplaned under the belly of the aircraft through the hole. The hole wasn't a circular hole in the Stirling, it was a coffin-shaped hole, oblong; and in the Stirling one was able to stand up, which was rather nice, but there were no seats. Seventeen entered the aircraft, in reverse order of our jumping out. I was to jump No 1 so I was the last in. Then the door was closed and we sat on the floor with our backs to the fuselage. It was quite dark inside the aircraft, there were only about six little red lights along the fuselage and there was nothing else to do except sit. We couldn't talk to each other because the engines started up, roared away and we taxied around. With about five minutes to go, we all moved up closer. I was astride the door, looking down at the sea and I hoped to see some of the task force, some of the armada, but I didn't see any ships at all, just the speckly wave tops of the sea below me.

Suddenly I saw the parallel lines of waves coming ashore on the dark yellow beach and then a cliff and woods and copses and hedgerows, only about 800 feet below me. It was a moonlit night so I could see the ground quite easily. Then - red light on, green light and I jumped. The roar of the engine, the whish of the wind around one's body and then quietness. Just like on an exercise in England, I found myself floating down to a field just to the side of a grazing horse. I landed without any harm. Having got out of my harness I reckoned that I'd been dropped on the right spot and I shouted for any men who happened to be landing around me and could hear me. I gathered up a little group of four and together with my compass we marched off westwards towards the rendezvous. The 7th Battalion had a bugle to rendezvous their lads in the copse on the edge of the dropping zone. The 13th Battalion had a hunting horn. But we, the 12th, had a red light. I got on to a little hillock on the dropping zone and flashed my torch around the area, hoping that our men would see the light and come towards me and then I'd despatch them to the battalion rendezvous in the quarry. Very few people came in during the hour that I was there.

'My company commander asked me to see if there were any Germans in four houses nearby, where we were going to establish our Battalion Headquarters. I took a sergeant and two soldiers and when we got to the first house I noticed there was a light on inside. I knocked and after probably about a minute, a middle-aged lady in her day clothes opened the door. At two o'clock in the morning this was a bit unusual. Behind her, her husband and two kids were also dressed in their day clothes. I said *'Bonjour Madame, nous sommes soldats d'Angleterre; nous arrivons ici par avion, parachutistes. L'heure de libération est arrivée. Ou sont les soldats allemands? Les soldats allemands restent ici?* She looked blankly at me. I was a dunce at French at school, but I thought I'd done quite well. I had another go but now she looked dazed and terrified - we were all camouflaged up with blackened faces. I then asked my sergeant, a right raw Yorkshireman, if he could speak French - he couldn't and neither could the other two, so I tried again. I'd barely started when she burst into tears, embraced me and said, 'You're British soldiers, aren't you?' So I said, 'Yes, I've been trying to tell you this for the last three or four minutes. You can speak English well, can't you?' 'Yes,' she said, 'I am English, born in Manchester and I married a French farmer before the war and settled here.' I asked her why it took her so long to come out with it. She explained that there had been Germans masquerading as British commandos or parachutists in the area to test them out. Then she said, 'It wasn't until I heard your frightful schoolboy French and your backchat to your sergeant that I realised that no German could possibly have acted the part!' She told us there were no Germans in the area.

'I went forward to establish what was known as a forward screen position on a hedgerow 300 yards in front of the company positions. We started to dig in to a hedgerow facing to the south, towards Caen and we had about an hour and a half of digging hard with our entrenching tools and the odd pick and shovel.

'It was a quiet morning. We noticed the RAF flying around above us, the odd aircraft with their white-striped wings giving us cover. We watched our front, being very still in our little holes, not moving. Then at about 11 o'clock that morning I noticed through my binoculars a group of about fifty soldiers debouching from a little copse about 400 yards in front of our positions. They looked very much like our own lads. They had round helmets on and camouflage smocks and I thought they were perhaps a group of our own parachute soldiers who had been dropped afar and were coming in to join us.

'This group moved across my front from left to right and then suddenly they deployed in extended line and advanced towards us through the fields, long grass, grass as high as the knee almost. We allowed them to come closer and closer. This was all part of our plan. They were enemy, I'd realised that: they were coming at us in a threatening manner and as they came closer one could see that they weren't British parachutists. There was a little cattle fence in front of us, going parallel to our hedgerow and we planned that until they reached the cattle fence we weren't going to open up on them. So they came closer and closer and when they reached the cattle fence I fired my red Very pistol straight at the middle of them and we all opened fire and the enemy went to ground.

'We engaged their fire for a little while and then ceased fire and I heard the sound of officers' orders, in German, working its way to my right, down towards the River Orne and I thought they were probably going to attack my position from the right side. There was a pause. We couldn't see any enemy to shoot at so we didn't shoot. And suddenly, to our surprise, two self-propelled guns came towards our position as if from nowhere, from dead ground in front of us. These two SP guns came side by side and stopped in front of our position about seventy yards away, short of the cattle fence and they started to systematically open fire on my positions and there was nothing we could do other than keep our heads down. I thought to myself, 'what a wonderful target for our six-pound anti-tank gun: point-blank range,' but nothing happened. And in the middle of this noise and the explosions a soldier came along the ditch from my anti-tank gun position, crawling up to me on his hands and knees. He saluted me on his hands and knees and he said, 'Sir, the gun's unserviceable, we can't get it to fire. It must have been damaged in the glider landing.' So I told him to go back to his position and open up with his personal weapon when he saw the enemy.

'I felt a bit numb. It was very terrifying and unusual to have bullets whipping over you and shells going off and there was such a lot of banging that they may have had some mortars opening up on our position too. There was a hell of a shindig around. But then, as happens in war, suddenly silence reigns: no more shooting; no more noise. And to my surprise one of the hatches on one of the SP guns in front of me opened up and out stepped a German officer arrayed in his service dress, belt, peaked hat, leather boots. He quietly got out and stood beside it and started to light a cigarette. He only had a couple of puffs, I think. Somebody in my section shot him and he fell to the ground and disappeared from sight. I don't think we killed him because later, when we walked round that area, there were no German officers' bodies lying around.

'Next, my sergeant, from the right-hand flank of my section, came up to me and said that he was the only one alive in his little area and he had run out of ammunition. What should we do? Well, there was no point in staying there any longer. I called out for any soldier around me who was alive to come and join me and I planned to get the hell out of it. There was my batman; he had a nasty gash in his cheek: he'd been shot in the face. There was a soldier on my right, dead, with his rifle up in his shoulder pointing towards the enemy. And after this call only this sergeant, my batman and two other soldiers came to me and I decided that the five of us would withdraw back to our positions. So this was what we did.

'I reported the situation to my company commander. Quietness remained in our hedgerow, there didn't seem to be any movement, so we decided to reoccupy the position. Another section from 'C' Company and I went back and we found that the enemy had withdrawn. There was no sign of any infantry. The two SP guns had moved out of their position and had gone round towards 'B' Company and I gather an hour or so later, both SP guns were shot and dispatched by the anti-tank guns of 'B' Company.

'So we were able to reoccupy the forward hedgerow position in peace. There were one or two wounded around. Our stretcher-bearers came up and we got our wounded back. I found myself at a loose end so what I decided to do was to remove the dead to Ranville church. Among them was a German soldier. While we were being mortared, this lone soldier had come down towards us carrying a rifle. I quietly said to my batman, 'Harris, you see that soldier coming down? Shoot him.' And he did. Much later I thought, 'How could I have given such an order?' I got a couple of soldiers from C Company and back in Le Bas de Ranville we found a handcart and then the three of us whipped this handcart up to the hedgerow position and we loaded up about four British soldiers including a sergeant, Sergeant Milburn and the German. And with these four or five dead we went with this handcart back into Ranville and I laid the dead along the cemetery wall by the church and returned to the company.'

For the rest of the day all was quiet and that evening the 1st Battalion of the Royal Ulster Rifles, which had landed from gliders with the rest of the Division, occupied Longueval. In the next day's fighting Private Hall of 'A' Company of the 12th Parachute Battalion particularly distinguished himself. Eight German Mark IV tanks were leading the attack from the south and one of the six-pounder anti-tank guns brought in by glider the evening before was standing silent, its crew dead around it. Hall loaded the gun, aimed it and knocked out two leading enemy tanks, firing but one round at each of them. He was about to dispose of the third when it received a mortar shell and blew up. The attack was repulsed and that evening the 12th Battalion of the Devonshire Regiment arrived by sea and took over the position.

During those two days, especially on the first of them, the 13th Parachute Battalion was heavily engaged, mostly by the 125th Panzer Grenadier Regiment, whose attacks were repulsed after fierce fighting in which for a time the position was very critical, since the Germans succeeded in forcing their way momentarily into Ranville; but at this juncture the hard-pressed parachute troops who, it should be remembered, because they had been scattered when dropped, had never been able to collect more than sixty per cent of their available strength, were reinforced by 1 Commando. The position was then held successfully.

Captain David Tibbs, Regimental Medical Officer, 13th Battalion, Parachute Regiment:
'The plane took off and one's pulse rate went up a little bit when you realised this was it. It was a Dakota, a twin-engined plane, with an open door on its side where we were going to jump so it was fairly noisy and there wasn't much opportunity for conversation. But most people were trying to rib each other a bit. Some chaps were a bit silent and looked a little bit green but really a general attitude of cheerfulness was kept up without any problems. I was tense and excited as I think anyone would be on this sort of occasion. It was my job as the officer in charge of the twenty men within the plane to keep up morale and not show any doubts but I think we all felt much the same.

'There was a blackout all over England so it was difficult to gauge where we were but we could judge when we were over the sea. I was sitting near the door of the plane so I could see down but really it was just blackness with the occasional burning embers of carbon from the engines coming back, which rather surprised me. At first I thought they were ack-ack shells coming up but they were little glowing embers off the aircraft engines.

'I was jumping No.1, standing at the door of the aircraft, when suddenly I saw to my horror another plane heading absolutely for us. The visibility was not very good so it must have been very close, it was a four-engined Stirling, which was one of the planes also involved in parachute dropping and glider tugging and what it was doing there I don't know, but we were clearly going to hit. At that point our pilot heeled right over to take evasive action and this plane did and by some miracle we did not hit each other. I glanced back at the men in the plane behind me and they had all been thrown to the floor, heavily laden men with parachutes all sprawling on the floor and one realised the difficulty they would have in getting out of the plane. The plane righted itself and immediately the green light came on warning us to jump. There was nothing I could do, I couldn't help the men behind me and so I jumped. But one didn't realise fully at the time the consequence of this. These men couldn't get upright with their heavy loads; they had to crawl to the door of the aircraft. And so, instead of jumping out one a second, because the aircraft was covering the ground at sixty yards a second they were spread out over a mile or two because they would be dropping every ten seconds, struggling to get out of the aircraft. So, as a consequence, many of these men we didn't see again. Only about five turned up on the dropping zone with me. Some were captured; others we didn't ever hear what had happened to them; others made their way back.

'There was a system of passwords and you had to give the appropriate reply. You might say 'B' and they would say 'Bulldog' in return. There was some confusion over this because each day had a different password; and of course the day before we had been geared up for the attack and now some people were still using the password for that day. In fact, I met, during the hours of darkness, one rather distressed journalist, because several journalists dropped with us, who'd got two Sten bullets in his neck. Fortunately he wasn't too badly hurt; they were just lodged under the skin. He had apparently given the wrong password or been misunderstood and been shot by our own men.

'My mission was to collect my men together and start rounding up any injured or wounded on the dropping zone and, when daylight came, to do a systematic search of the dropping zone, so, after I landed, I walked steadily in the direction of Ranville. In the distance I could hear the thump and crackle of the attack going on at the bridges over the river and canal about a mile away but apart from that it was extraordinarily quiet and I trudged along in the darkness for about a mile until I reached Ranville. I bumped into a few other men but considering that about two thousand men had dropped into this area at much the same time as myself it was extraordinary how few other people one met. Everyone was just making for their particular rendezvous points and various units were assembling, ready for their particular tasks.

'I think 68 gliders landed in quick succession on the dropping zone. One or two crash-landed but the great majority landed safely. This was very important because they were bringing a number of weapons we needed, such as anti-tank guns, both six-pounders and seventeen-pounders. The Germans didn't realise that we were able to bring down seventeen-pounder anti-tank guns, which were state of the art technology then and very much necessary for us. Also some light artillery came and a number of other heavy supplies of that sort. I went to one or two gliders where there had been crashes. One or two people had been killed. I retrieved some of the injured there. One of my chaps had been very resourceful and had got a gas-driven wagon belonging to the French and that was very helpful in lifting out these people and taking them back to Le Bas de Ranville, where the medical centre was being established.

'When daybreak came, I had five men with me. This was rather upsetting because I'd hoped to have twenty, but we started a systematic search now that it was day. One unexpected thing was that most of the dropping zone was wheat, about two to three feet high, so that a man lying badly injured on the ground was very difficult to see because he was just buried in wheat, but we did our best to cover the ground. Many of the injured we had to collect were men with fractured femurs. It was quite interesting how this had occurred: they had all dropped with their kit bags still attached to their legs.

'A number of men portrayed their presence when they realised we weren't far away by waving anything they could find up in the air. We would see a hand waving and realise there was somebody there and we would immediately go over and rescue him. My main memory of this was the sheer physical exertion of carrying these men by stretcher. Two of us carrying a stretcher, perhaps carrying him up to mile over the ground is very hard work indeed and that is where we missed the full squad of twenty men.

'The gliders and lots of helmets were still lying on the dropping zone and lots of gas masks had been discarded, so it was covered in litter. But apart from that, during the morning of D-Day, this particular dropping zone was almost deserted. All the troops, British and German, were keeping well out of sight in houses and woods and so on and I was left comparatively unmolested. I was wearing and so were my men, Red Cross armlets, so we were fairly easily distinguished as medical people and although a few shots and a certain amount of mortars were fired in our direction we were left to get on with our task without too much disturbance.

'Dawn broke. It was rather misty and we could see the coast from where we were. Then about half past six or onwards one of my men called out and pointed and I looked towards the sea and there you could see, emerging out of the mist, a large number of craft. This was about two to three miles away so they were only small dots but it was a tremendous boost to our morale to see all this coming in. From then on there was a continuous rumbling from the coastal areas of the attack going on there, which was a great spur to us.

'Fierce fighting was going around while the Germans tried to recapture the bridges over the canal and the river and Le Bas de Ranville itself was almost in the front line. The Germans were only a few hundred yards away from Le Bas de Ranville and attacking it fiercely all the time, just as Ranville itself was under counter-attack from the Germans who were beginning to send in elements of the 21st Panzer Division.

'The scene around the Field Ambulance, which was occupying a château in Le Bas de Ranville, was extraordinary. We were, the 5th Parachute Brigade, by this stage confined to a very tight area in Ranville and Le Bas de Ranville and the Germans were fiercely attacking, which meant there were constant storms of mortars coming down and a number of casualties occurring all the time. In the Field Ambulance itself, a large number, perhaps a hundred or two wounded, had been brought in and were filling the main building and outlying buildings including a barn, many of them desperately wounded. The surgeons were doing their best to cope with some of the worst wounded who would benefit most; for example, those with haemorrhage or thoracic wounds. The scene was one of noise, of wounded men, but nevertheless of organisation. People were going about ignoring all the mortar fire, though casualties were occurring within the Field Ambulance. Our own batteries of mortars were firing off from just about a hundred yards away so the noise was continual and heavy and casualties were rolling in all the time.

'As the afternoon wore on, I was put in charge of a barn containing nearly a hundred wounded men. I did my best for them. It was filled with hay, which was in a way fortunate for them to lie on. But in the late afternoon there was a sudden moment of panic as somebody threw open the door to the barn and said, 'The Germans are here! They're just at the bottom of the road!' And one of the wounded, a sergeant, who up till that time had looked too ill to do anything, partially sat up, grabbed his Sten gun which was lying beside him and swore violently at this man and said in a broad Glaswegian accent, 'Stop your blethering, man. Or ye'll be the first to go!' I then noticed, to my horror, that not only was the hay a big incendiary risk but most of the wounded still had their weapons with them and they were quite prepared to fight and if the Germans did overrun us we wouldn't stand a chance. I myself was carrying a pistol. But while I was standing there, things settled down. The tank that was coming in with these Germans was knocked out and that particular scare was over.

'It was tremendous spectacle to see these coming in, the gliders circling round to find their way down safely to the ground and the planes passing on and as they did so dropping these huge tow ropes, incidentally, on to the Germans. This was a tremendous morale booster. The extraordinary thing was how little ack-ack fire they encountered and how everything went silent, both the Germans and ourselves who were watching this extraordinary spectacle, which was a tremendous boost for us but no doubt the very reverse for the Germans. The wonderful thing was that the great majority of these gliders came down exactly as planned. They were bringing desperately needed anti-tank guns and about 1,500 glider-borne infantry and a number of other weapons and communications equipment and another Field Ambulance.

'Well, the evening wore on and at about half-past ten we learned that casualties could be evacuated. So carefully selected people, selected because they were near death but salvable if they were given proper help, were evacuated by jeep-ambulances across the bridges to join the main dressing station the other side of the river. This was a hazardous journey because they were liable to be mortared or sniped at all along this route. Anyway, evacuation had started and we were beginning to have real communications with the seaborne people.

'By midnight, although it was rather like the aftermath of the Battle of Waterloo with the Field Ambulance full of wounded, morale was high. During the night it was relatively quiet but we knew the dawn would bring a storm of fire again and further fighting and further casualties, as indeed happened. But we ended the day with great confidence that we were going to succeed. Obviously fear was by our side but with it was a great determination to see things through. I can only speak with the greatest of praise for the fighting men outside who were defending the perimeter and determined to hold everything they had obtained so far. We were very tired but in a way exultant, because we knew that we had got the better of the situation and all the objectives that we had really wanted and were going for had been obtained and if only we could hold on we should succeed.'

Those of the 3rd Parachute Brigade under Brigadier James S. Hill DSO MC like the 5th had three main tasks. It was their duty to capture and destroy an enemy battery at Merville and to demolish the bridges at Troarn, Bures, Robehomme and Varaville over the River Dives and the numerous waterways connected with it. Finally, they were to deny to the enemy the use of any roads leading into the area from the south and east. Much of their task was in the nature of a roving commission and in fulfilling it they were performing one of the main duties of airborne troops, which is to harass the enemy, disrupt his communications and create a condition of alarm and despondency in the areas immediately behind his forward troops.

Brigadier James Hill DSO MC Commanding Officer, 3rd Parachute Brigade:
'I wanted my brigade to go to church at least once a month, but some didn't like this very much. So to motivate them I made them carry 60 pounds of equipment to church, which they stacked up outside under guard before going inside. After the service I would take them for a 20-mile march. I thought that might motivate them to enjoy their time at church a bit more! A number of people told me later what a difference those church visits had made. When we were crossing the North Sea on D-Day it was a pretty rough night and sitting in those planes were men of 22 who had never seen a shot fired in anger and were now flying into enemy territory. Up against something like that, even an atheist wanted to pray.

'I was jumping No. 1, which gave me a problem. In camp, to keep the Canadians amused, I'd given them a football with Hitler's face on it in luminous paint. Everyone knew I was proposing to drop this, along with three bricks, which they gave me with some rather vulgar wording painted on them, on to the beach to astonish the enemy. So there I was, as brigade commander, standing in the door of the aeroplane with a football and three bricks! As we got over the beaches, out went the football and the bricks and myself.

'It was an inaccurate landing, but it could have been worse. As I orientated myself, it appeared that I had been dropped with my stick bang in the middle of the River Dives. However, what the Germans had done in anticipation was to flood the valley. On either side of the river were water meadows with irrigation ditches; some of them 14 feet deep. With 60 pounds of equipment, falling into a ditch like that would have meant going down. The Germans had wired this area before they flooded it so they had really created a very impenetrable barrier. The landing was inaccurate because the pilots who flew us over to Normandy had been bomber pilots until about six weeks before D-Day. They had been used to bombing cities from 10,000 feet, now they had to drop paratroops from 700 feet onto a drop zone about 1,000 metres square. I had suspected that the drops might be inaccurate and had said to my men some weeks before, 'Gentlemen, in spite of your excellent training and very clear orders, don't be daunted if chaos reigns - because it certainly will.'

'I dropped a quarter of a mile from Cabourg where the Dives enters the sea and close to the River Dives in four feet of water. I had a four-hour struggle to reach dry land near our own dropping zone. During that period, to my annoyance, I found myself making tea: being a good soldier I always had teabags sewn in my battledress and, of course, dropping in four feet of water, I left a stream of cold tea behind me. And when I was still in the water I heard shots and I thought, 'By God, here we are, we're getting into battle at once.' When I investigated, it was one member of my bodyguard shooting the other one in the leg by mistake, thinking he was a German.

'I collected forty-two soaking wet stragglers, who included two parachute-sailors[1] and an Alsatian parachuting dog[2] and we tied ourselves together with our toggle ropes. It meant we were all in control and if we came across wire under water, we were all there to deal with it. As we walked it was getting light and we were in a very narrow track with no ditches and there was water on the other side of the hedge. Suddenly I heard a horrible noise. I'd seen fighting before and I knew it was pattern bombing by low-flying aircraft. So I shouted to the chaps to get down, we all flung ourselves down. I flung myself on my friend Lieutenant Peters the 9th Battalion mortar platoon commander. I thought to myself, 'This is it' and I knew I'd been hit. All you were aware of was dust and the smell of death. It was horrible. Then I looked to my left and in the middle of the path I saw a leg and I thought, 'By God, that's my leg.' I had another look at it and I realised it wasn't because it had a brown boot on it. I had a strict rule that no one in my brigade was to wear brown boots, which were American parachute boots. But I was lying on Peters, the only person who broke that rule and who was dead. It was his leg. I'd had much of my left backside removed but otherwise I was OK.

'The dead and injured were all around us. I was faced with the choice: do I stay and look after the injured, or do I press on? As brigade commander I had a great responsibility, so I had to press on. Before leaving we took the morphine from the dead and gave it to the living. We set off and the injured chaps gave us a cheer. That memory is as vivid today as it ever was.

'I staggered to my feet and I could only see one other person who was able to get up and that was my defence platoon commander. So, the first problem of a commander: what do I do? I was surrounded by dead and dying chaps. Do I look after them or do I get on with business? And of course the answer was, you have to get on with business. My mother was a soldier's wife and at the outbreak of war she said to me, 'Darling, if you're going to survive this war, you've got to learn to harden your heart.' That was good advice. You could have a hard heart and still have compassion and I was full of compassion for the people I left there. But as commander, I had to go where my most important task lay. So with my defence platoon commander I went round all the bodies that were dead and took their morphine off them and we handed the morphine to the living, so they at least had that little bit of comfort and then there was nothing for it but to leave them. It was a ghastly sight. I shall never forget and it will haunt me

1   Royal Navy personnel who dropped with the airborne forces to provide a wireless link with the naval bombardment force offshore.
2   'From January 1943 until D-Day we had to keep the chaps interested and on top form. One of the things I introduced in order to do that was parachuting dogs. A team of paratroops were trained in handling Alsatian messenger dogs. The dogs were given bicycle parachutes, as they were roughly the same weight as bicycles. The first time we took one of the dogs up he didn't want to jump, so we shoved him out. It turns out he enjoyed himself so much that the next time he couldn't wait to go! The dogs were trained to be messengers, but they were really just a sideshow to keep the men amused.'

to my dying day that as the two of us moved on they all gave us a cheer and wished us luck. I don't think any of them lived to tell the tale. The Germans threw the bodies of those chaps into a big shell hole, but a few days later we captured the area and unearthed them and gave them each a proper burial.

'I arrived at the foot of the Le Plein feature and found the 9th Battalion and was told that they'd been successful and had silenced the guns in the Merville battery. Then I was seized upon by Doc Watts. He hustled me into his regimental aid post and he took a look at me and said, 'You look bad for morale.' So I looked at him and I said, 'You bloody fellow. If you'd been in four feet of water and had your left backside removed you wouldn't look good for morale. And it's your job to do something about it.' (I learned afterwards that his reaction was, 'By George, I've got a difficult case on my hands. I'll put him out.' So he injected me and I was out for a couple of hours and while I was out he patched up my wounds.) As I lay there waiting for my operation at about 1pm, I heard a dense shelling and thought to myself, 'I hope that the British will still be here when I come to and not a lot of Germans.' When I came to at about 3pm I was told that I was the first person to be given penicillin, which had just been invented. I had a bottle strapped to my side and attached to it were tubes that carried penicillin dripping into my wounds. It was rather undignified - half my backside and my trousers shot away and as brigade commander I usually liked to keep up a bit of style.

'We got into a jeep to drive to brigade headquarters, with me balancing myself on my right side. We got there at about 4pm. Alistair Pearson, one of the greatest fighting battalion commanders of the war, had taken command of the brigade in my absence. He was OK apart from having been shot through the hand.

'I was sitting on the top of the steps that led to an outdoor barn where I had my personal headquarters and I smelled to high heaven because I'd developed gangrene. I was very unapproachable, really. As a brigade commander going into battle, you have a beautiful map case and sharp pencils, but there I was, minus half my backside, minus a pair of trousers and all our chaps were in exactly the same boat. It was go, guts and gumption. I looked away to the north-west and seeing the arrival of an airlanding brigade into battle. It was a wonderful sight. Hundreds and hundreds of gliders coming in. So we knew we weren't going to be alone. I said to myself, 'Remember all these things, because you're never going to see a sight like this again.'

'I knew they were carrying supplies and the sight of them coming in to land made me feel less lonely, just as the sounds of the dawn battle had that morning. It was a great relief to know that we'd got to France, we had captured our objectives and we were exactly where we were supposed to be. We knew we still had a fight on our hands, but we had landed. We had a little bit of France and those gliders coming in to land were following us. The battle started from there. Not with beautiful clean clothes and a nice map case, but worn out, wet, dirty and smelly.

Signalman Harry Read, 3rd Parachute Brigade:

'Shortly after we arrived in our field and had settled into our tents we were assembled to learn the strategy of the campaign and to learn the precise parts we were to play. It was a very sobering experience. Whatever feelings of exultation any of us might have had were punctured as we were briefed. It was clear from the briefing that very substantial casualties were expected on the landing itself. No wonder our section had such a generous supply of wireless operators! The casualty expectation looked to be in the region of 50%. If others thought as I thought, the prospect of a safe return home was diminishing by the minute but, having put our lives on the line there was no thought of backing out, we would sell our lives dearly. We were all in the same boat and we trusted each other to do our jobs well.

'We were supposed to take-off on the night our fourth June and were all geared for that. I think it was during the afternoon that word came to the effect that the weather conditions were severe and the campaign was put off for another 24 hours. At least, it gave a lot of men another 24 hours of living. The next day, the fifth, we boarded the transports and were driven to the airfield. The RAF treated us very kindly. They gave us a slap-up meal of bangers and mash after which we trooped out to the airfield where all the aircraft were lined up awaiting us. They looked very, very impressive. They were American Dakotas - C-47s. I am guessing that it was about 10pm when we emplaned having been hanging about for a very long time. Getting a whole brigade into aircraft and airborne is a time consuming task but, eventually, we roared off the runway and were airborne, Getting a fleet like that into formation before heading for the battlefield was time consuming also and, after stooging round and round seemingly for hours, we set off for France. Our time of destiny had arrived. An interesting moment came when the pilot spoke on the intercom inviting us to look down to view the coastline informing us that we were passing over Poole Bay.

'Quite how long it took us to reach the French Coast I do not know, but we had the command to stand, hook up our parachutes and check the chute of the man in front. Our aircraft lurched drunkenly upwards and we wondered what had caused it. Over the intercom came the pilot's voice telling us that he had released two large anti-personnel bombs 'just to keep the enemy's heads down'. We were reassured but he might have forewarned us. The aircraft moved into a significantly slower, steady course, the red light came on, then the green and we were moving as quickly as possible to the exit. We were so cluttered with kit that we needed help to reach the door and get out and the despatcher did not fail us. The roar of the engine increased as we left the plane and we were battered by the slipstream before our chutes opened - our war had truly begun.

'The descent was interesting. There was no throat-swelling fear, just the awareness of what had to be done. The sky was alive and alight with shells, tracer bullets and noise from the explosions and yet we felt - I felt - an air of detachment. In the distance an aircraft plunged to the earth in a ball of fire and then, I landed. If that is the right word to use because between me and the land was a couple of feet of water. It was an unexpectedly soft landing.

'I had landed in the area, west of the River Dives that the Germans had flooded with water to discourage airborne troops. It was a successful ploy on their part. When daylight came we could see the silk circles on top of the water indicating that a parachutist had descending and drowned before he could free himself from his harness. It was a salutary sight.

'The plan outlined to us in the concentration area was that, on landing, we would look for a strong green light and rendezvous on it. Lights there were in plenty but not one that looked remotely like a rendezvous light. I thought I had better move through the water in the general direction of our flight. Picking up the heavy wooden-sided accumulator I had jumped with, I put it on my shoulder and fell straight into a trench full of flood-water. With much difficulty I extricated myself remembering that, before flooding, the Germans had dug trenches across the land to add further hazards to their defences. Another few paces and again, I virtually disappeared and had to scramble out. This was to happen frequently but, on the third occasion, I concluded that the accumulator had become a pointless burden so I tipped it back into the ditch and continued walking. We had landed fairly near to a village called Robhomme but we were further east than we should have been, hence the flooded area.

'Shortly after this I met another man from my aircraft. He was a member of the defence platoon and I knew him only as Paddy. We plodded on together for a while and met another little group that had an artillery Captain in charge. It was still quite dark and when they said which way they were going Paddy and I were not impressed and continued our own way. We waded through water both deep and shallow. Occasionally we were shot at, but we must have been bad targets as we continued towards Robhomme. In the afternoon we came to a knoll with a few trees offering shelter. We valued the opportunity to dry out a little, have a meal and keep under observation a farmhouse that looked as if it might be valuable to us. When we had witnessed no movement for a time, we walked towards the farmhouse - again we had to go through some water and when we reached the door, Paddy knocked while I covered him with my Sten gun. The door opened and the warmest of welcomes awaited us from the farmer and his family. In the large living room there must have been twenty to thirty other airborne troops present, as was the village priest.

'The priest had just arrived and counselled us to stay put. To move in any direction would, in his judgment, be foolhardy. He told us that nearer to Robhomme there was another group of Paras. He promised to contact them and tell them about us. We slept well that night on the straw in the barn and the next day the priest returned to say that someone would come to us from that other group and give us instructions. The priest had not been gone long before a Sergeant came along· a Sergeant who was very anxious to let it be known that he was in charge - but the message was that later that night someone would come for us, would lead us to the other group and that all together, we would journey to le Mesnil which was the proposed place for the headquarters of our 3rd Parachute Brigade. In due course, we made our way towards the other group and we were formed up into a single file. The people they didn't particularly trust with firearms - namely we headquarters lot - they stuck in the middle while the infantrymen were fore and aft and we made what seemed to be a very, very long journey during that night.

'It was a potentially hazardous journey because every now and again the column shuffled to a halt and there was gunfire either front or back. Then the command came to advance and we would go past a vehicle containing the bodies of the Germans who had just been killed.

'Early in the morning - five or six o'clock - we linked up with our own units. Paddy and I just walked into the 3 Para Brigade headquarters both of us amazed at the small number of men there. We had expected a greater number. Chaps I didn't know wonderfully well, even though we were in the same section, greeted me like a long-lost brother. I guess we lost at least a third of our men - not all killed, of course. Some would be wounded; some prisoners, some 'just missing' and one or two like ourselves straggled in after us. The losses were not good and that radio set we had packed with such care and were supposed to operate never did appear. We lost so much equipment it was unbelievable.

'Our Brigade Headquarters was set up in a farm - a working farm still despite the fact that it was now in the front line. The Signal Office was in a small barn. Next to it was a larger barn that was used as a mortuary and next to that, a large barn which became a Field Hospital where a team of medics, tirelessly, compassionately and skilfully attended to the wounded. A field just down to the right became a temporary burial ground. In our cramped, dark and somewhat smelly Signal office we had our field telephone exchange and the Brigade wireless set.

'When, in August we were able to break out of our entrenched position, I was one of those assigned to work on the roving set that accompanied the Brigade Commander, Brigadier James Hill. So, I either trudged along behind him with one those wretched voice-only wirelesses on my back or, when we had the luxury of the jeep, we used the decent set installed in the rear. The Brigadier was a very brave man and a superb soldier.'

'Our primary role was to destroy three bridges, one at Troarn and two at Bures. We had to hold Troarn as long as possible. We were then to withdraw to our main position. This we were to hold, there was to be no withdrawal without orders from the Divisional commander.

'We landed at ten minutes to 1 am on 6 June. I had a good DZ, K, about 3-4 kilometres from Troarn. The drop was a shambles. Instead of having 600-700 people within half an hour of landing, I had about 100.

'...Practically everyone was out on patrol every night to give the enemy the impression that we were very strong - which we were not - and to keep the enemy off balance. It is easy to knock the German off his stride. If you disorganise him, he finds it hard to reorganise. You have to keep on hitting him, not necessarily cause many casualties - just keep at him.'

Lieutenant Colonel Alistair Pearson DSO MC, 8th Parachute Battalion.**

The 1st Canadian Parachute Battalion dropped in the general area round the villages of Varaville and Robehomme on the River Dives. Their task was to destroy the bridges at those places and, though they were widely scattered, they did so successfully without much opposition and subsequently held a position not far from the Bois de Bavent.

'Here we were, 'C' Company, just over 100 of us, taking off in little bombers to drop behind Hitler's 'impregnable Atlantic Wall' and take on Rommel's soldiers. We were perfectly aware that attacking infantry should have a three-to-one ratio in its favour, but according to intelligence reports we were going in to do our job at close on one-to-one. We were loaded to the hilt with grenades, Gammon bombs, flexible Bangalore torpedoes around our necks, two-inch mortar bombs, ammunition, weapons and water bottles. Our exposed skin was blackened with charcoal, the camouflage netting on our helmets was all tied up with burlap rags and the space above the harnesses in our helmets was crammed with cigarettes or with plastic explosive.

   'A few minutes before the drop, we passed over a town where the streets, a few hundred feet below, were full of promenading people. That was the toughest moment of all, for each of us knew that we might never have the chance to do something like that, ever again. Somebody said, 'For Chrissakes gimme a cigarette,' to which the sergeant growled, 'You know better'n that - stow the cigarettes 'til after Varaville.'
Corporal Dan Hartigan 1st Canadian Parachute Battalion.

The 8th Parachute Battalion, whose task it was to destroy the two bridges over the same river at Bures and the bridge at Troarn, had more difficulty. Two and a half hours after the drop, its Commanding Officer, Lieutenant-Colonel R. S. Pearson DSO MC had only succeeded in collecting 120 all ranks. Among them were no Royal Engineers or machine-gunners and there were explosives enough to destroy only two of the three bridges. He moved first on those at Bures. In the meantime a detachment of Royal Engineers had landed on the northern outskirts of the Bois de Bavent. They collected a satisfactory quantity of explosive and demolition equipment from the kitbags and container loads dropped with them and moved off in two parties, one marching towards Bures, dragging their equipment with them on trolleys, the other making for the more distant Troarn in a jeep.

'I was dressed in what was jocularly called 'Christmas Tree order' because one's parachute harness had to be sufficiently tight to stop it being jerked off one's shoulders when the chute opened. As a consequence, I could barely walk in an upright position. Strapped up in this way, I had a .45 Colt automatic, a Sten gun through my harness and a cartridge-pistol. On the run in to Normandy, the flak started to come up and when the pilot started to jink, I fell flat on my back in the doorway of the Dakota plane and it took two men to lift me to my feet again. This was despite the fact that we'd been briefed that we would go into Normandy on a flak-less route. In actual fact, the Germans were on an anti-invasion exercise in the very area in which we were to land. The man who said that he wasn't scared when he did a parachute jump was a liar, because every jump one did had its attendant nervous tension - but on this occasion we had the strain of going into battle for the first time.'

Captain Dennis Kelland, 8th Parachute Battalion, Regiment, landing east of River Orne.

The first party soon fell in with the reconnaissance party of the 8th Parachute Battalion, who covered them while, according to plan, they destroyed the two bridges. The Sappers in the jeep going to Troarn, Major J. C. A. 'Rosie' Roseveare and seven other ranks, travelled at high speed, their Bren and Sten guns at the ready. At a level crossing near the town they ran into a barbed wire knife-rest and it took them twenty minutes to cut themselves and their vehicle free. Though by that time the German garrison had been thoroughly aroused, the Sappers would not be turned from their task. Putting on full speed, they rushed through the town firing their Sten guns, Sapper Peachey acting as a rear-gunner and making excellent practice. Immediately beyond Troarn the road falls steeply. Down the hill sped the jeep under a hail of machine-gun bullets, all of them fortunately flicking just above the heads of its occupants. The bridge was reached and five minutes later a gap twenty feet wide had been blown in it. The jeep was then ditched and the party moved on foot to a rendezvous at Le Mesnil.

Major 'Rosie' Roseveare, Royal Engineers who was given the task of destroying a bridge at Troarn:
'When we were getting near, beggar me if we didn't run smack into a barbed-wire barricade across the road. By the time I saw it, it was too late. We couldn't ram it, because barbed wire is hopeless stuff and gets wrapped round everything, but by the grace of God one of our chaps had some wire-cutters with him and he cut us out. We stopped short of a crossroads at the edge of town and I sent a couple of chaps forward to look round the corner and here a really farcical situation developed. While they were looking in one direction, a German soldier appeared on a bicycle from the other direction. Well, I suppose in hindsight we should have stuck a knife in the chap, but what happened was that someone shot at him and that really set things going.

'All we could do was jump aboard the jeep and make the best pace we could. I suppose we had about half a ton of explosives in the trailer and there were seven of us on the jeep, with me driving, so we couldn't make very high speed. As we came into the centre of the town, the firing started from various windows and from the ground as well; there seemed to be a Boche in every doorway firing like mad. Our chaps were firing back. One German rushed out with an MG34 and put it down in the road, but we were too quick for him and he had to whip it out of the way or we would have run him over. But he was terribly quick getting it out again and a stream of tracer went over our heads. The only thing that saved us was that there was a steep downward hill leading out of Troarn and he couldn't depress his gun far enough.

'We raced down the hill, picking up speed all the time and I nearly lost control of the darn thing. There was an appalling swerve and I think that's where we lost one of our men, our Bren gunner, when he fell off the trailer.

'When we got to the bridge it took us less than five minutes to set all the charges across the centre of the biggest arch and down she went. Obviously we couldn't go back through the town; we were definitely persona non grata there, so we took to the fields and finally arrived back at brigade headquarters. On the way we passed a farmer milking a cow and I told him in French that liberation was at hand. He was most unimpressed.'

'The further we went the more fire there was and the faster Roseveare drove the Jeep. I was sitting at the front, blazing away with my Sten gun at anything that moved. One German with a machine gun rushed into the road to really have a go at us and changed his mind because he got the hell out of it. Roseveare was driving like mad, zig-zagging from side to side.'
22-year-old Sergeant Bill Irving, Royal Engineers.

Throughout the day many other sappers arrived at that place, having had a number of brisk encounters with the enemy. Some had landed close to Ranville and been made prisoner for a time. But not for long: one of them, Sergeant Jones, snatched a Schmeisser from a German and with it killed eight of his captors. Another, Sapper Thomas, though wounded while still in the air, on landing wiped out with grenades a party of three who had been shooting at him. One aircraft took such violent evasive action that the parachutists in it were thrown flat and fell out one by one, at intervals, the stick stretching from Varaville to Robehomme, a distance of two miles. At both these places the bridges were successfully destroyed. In the British Army the Royal Engineers enjoy a reputation for courageous eccentricity. It was enhanced that day by Captain A. J. Jack, who, having blown the bridge at Robehomme, sat down with his men, cooked and ate breakfast, heedless of the warnings volunteered by the local inhabitants that the enemy might appear at any moment. Such coolness did much to inspire the French and increase the already high fighting qualities of his men.

While these sappers were blowing the bridges, others had dropped on the landing zone chosen for the gliders in which the Brigade and Divisional Headquarters, together with a certain quantity of anti-tank guns, were being carried.' The fields forming the zone had been partially obstructed by poles. These, the sappers soon removed and then set about laying out the landing strips. The lights upon them proved difficult to see and when the gliders came in 'some passed each other within thirty feet, going in opposite directions, but with the traditional ability of the Horsa to take punishment, casualties were very few.' The two airborne bulldozers carried were particularly useful. One of them broke through the floor of its glider but safely survived the subsequent crash to the ground and both machines were working on strips within an hour of landing. In eight hours, which was well within the margin of time allotted, they had cleared the four strips of glider debris and filled in the holes which had been dug by the enemy to receive poles. Their operators worked without pause or intermission, all the time under sniper, mortar and shell fire.

The confused nature of that night's happenings is well illustrated by the adventures of an anonymous captain, the first to jump from his aircraft. He landed alone in the middle of the River Dives, climbed out and reached a farm, where he picked up four parachute soldiers. A young French boy undertook to lead them to their destination, Varaville, which they reached about 3.30 in the morning. 'Complete chaos seemed to reign in the village. Against a background of Brens, Spandaus and grenades could be heard the shouts of British and Canadians, Germans and Russians. There was obviously a battle in progress. The captain and his party determined to make for Le Mesnil, where he knew the Brigade was to establish a firm base. An Englishwoman, a cockney from Camberwell, about fifty-five years old, then made her appearance and explained what was wanted to their young French guide. On the way to Le Mesnil they entered a wood and had a brush with a German patrol. One of the enemy threw a stick grenade which burst on the French boy's head and killed him. The party had now lost their guide, 'their maps were not fit to use and they had already tramped for two miles through swamps with the water often chest high.'

After a time they fell in with some French farmers who gave them fresh milk and bread. It was now light and for all that day the party, swollen to about twenty, moved through the fields and through the Bois de Bavent. By four o'clock in the afternoon, after they had crossed a number of canals twenty feet deep and 'were all completely whacked' they saw the gliders carrying the rest of the Division coming in to land. 'This exhilarating sight revived their spirits, which soared still higher when they saw some Spitfires... bring a couple of Messerschmitts down into the swamp quite close to them. They struggled on, not daring to rest in the swamp for fear of drowning.' By ten in the evening they reached terra firma at last, having taken six hours to cover two miles through the swamp. They had still not reached Le Mesnil but were eventually put on the right road by 'a very drunken Frenchman.'

The plan for the store-carrying gliders was that they should land, some on each of the dropping zones, a short time before the arrival of the parachutists. Like the gliders, which took part in the attack on the battery at Merville, all those ordered to land on the dropping zones experienced bad weather conditions, accentuated by, the huge clouds of smoke and dust caused by bombing. About half the gliders detailed to land north of Petiville did so successfully, though their unloading took a long time. Those landing between Toufreville and Cuverville were less fortunate, only one-third reaching their destination, the remainder, save for one which was lost, landing on another dropping zone. The third group of gliders was to land between Ranville and Amfreville in the area nearest the vital bridges over the Orne and the Caen Canal and close to the spot which had been chosen for Divisional Headquarters. Here a high measure of success was attained, for forty-nine out of the seventy-two gliders which took off landed according to plan. Five made forced landings in the United Kingdom, three in the sea and fourteen were lost.

Once on the ground the glider pilots, fighting as a unit, were soon in action. By the evening ninety-three, composing 'Force John;' were well dug in and defending the zone from the south-west. One of them, Captain B. Murdoch, presently found himself involved in a brisk action against tanks. He was acting as leader at the time to a six-pounder anti-tank gun, of which the layer was killed. Captain Murdoch took over and he and the other gunners succeeded in destroying four out of five enemy tanks.

Of the fourteen gliders which failed to reach their destination, one, piloted by Major J. F. Lyne, was hit by flak in the tail when crossing the coast and the tow rope broke. The glider was in cloud and immediately began to descend.

On coming out into clear air it was again hit, a shell bursting in the centre of the fuselage and damaging the jeep on board, but hurting no one. Beneath was darkness shot with fire and to choose a suitable spot on which to land was even more difficult than usual. The glider sailed remorselessly earthward and at the last moment a pale patch, which 'seemed to be a little less dark than the rest of the countryside,' loomed up. It was an orchard and into it Major Lyne crashed his glider, breaking his foot and cutting the face of his second pilot. These were the only mishaps: The party of seven set off, their one object being to find someone who could tell them where they were. They soon ran into Germans, lay up in a field till dawn and then found a farmer who directed them towards the River Dives. This they swam and joined up with some Canadian parachute troops isolated near Robehomme. By then they were entirely surrounded by the enemy and it took them three days to reach Ranville. Throughout that time the French inhabitants were of the greatest help and their grape-vine information service enabled Lyne and his men to know at all times the exact position of the enemy. During their wanderings they met with a farm labourer and his family who produced as evidence of their love of England 'a portrait of Queen Victoria tastefully executed in Nottingham lace' and provided them with a meal, a map torn from a school atlas and two pocket dictionaries.

Eventually Major Lyne and the rest entered the Bois de Bavent and there, though exhausted by forty-eight hours of stumbling through swampy ground, hiding in ditches, swimming streams and thrusting their way through unyielding undergrowth, reached at long last a road running in the right direction. At that moment the enemy appeared. The weary men went at once into action with their personal weapons. 'We managed to eliminate two lorry-loads of Germans and a car with four officers in it,' reports Major Lyne, 'by the simple process of throwing hand grenades at them. They were all wiped out. By this time we were all very tired.' When they eventually reached the landing zone, after another fight, they had marched forty-five miles from the place where the glider had landed.

Men like these and their comrades, stubbornly holding the boundaries of the landing zones, made possible that mass landing of gliders on the evening of the first day which had been watched so thankfully by Private

Owen from his slit trench on the bank of the Caen Canal. Every Hamilcar carrying the heavy stores and 112 out of 114 Horsas, landed according to plan and from them poured the remainder of the Division, consisting of the 6th Air Landing Brigade and a number of other units including the Armoured Reconnaissance Regiment. The success of this operation is the best tribute to those who had first shown on the dusty fields of Sicily what skill and gallantry can achieve in the handling of a new and hazardous vehicle for the carriage of troops to battle.

'I prepared for D-Day by doing my glider training at Brize Norton, but when 6 June finally arrived they had run out of gliders, so we went across the Channel by boat. Luckily for us, the Royal Navy and the RAF had done a good job. They made-our landing at Arromanches fairly straight-forward with little resistance. The crossing had been plenty rough but I was advised to keep eating - however sick I felt - and it worked. The captain of our landing craft got as near to the coast as possible but we still got a soaking. I was one of the most popular members of our platoon and the only one with dry cigarettes. I had put them in my helmet. Not only that, I didn't smoke. The real fighting started a few miles inland. We were to be involved in some fierce battles and we lost a lot of men. I saw some terrible, terrible things. Things you never forget.

'I received a head wound but refused to stay in hospital; a big mistake on my part as we were shelled most of the night. In battles that followed, I was hit by a piece of shrapnel, but it lodged in the mess tins I was carrying with me. They saved me. But my platoon sergeant was blown to pieces just yards away from me and my company commander was also killed. I was one of eight out of 22 in our platoon who survived. I was very lucky. Someone was looking over me.'

Len Mann, who when he was 18 joined the 12th Battalion of the Devonshire Regiment who 'turned him into a soldier'. Previously he had been a trainee butcher at Sainsbury's in Norwich. He went on an anti-tank gun course and then became part of the 6th Airborne Division Air Landing Brigade, flying gliders. After returning to England and getting some home leave he returned to France and then, in the final assault, was in a glider that crossed the Rhine at Hamekelem. 'I crash-landed. Snipers were firing at us, but once again I was lucky. Some of my comrades weren't. I saw four men burned alive. Dreadful. They never stood a chance. We carried on into Germany and eventually victory was ours. It had been a long, hard and bloody struggle. When I was returned to England, the driver of the vehicle fell asleep and hit a tree at Calais. I ended my fracturing my hip and couldn't walk for several months - and that was the end of my war.'

So by the end of the first two days, the 6th Airborne Division was established firmly on the eastern bank of the River Orne, holding a half-circle round the little villages of Ranville, Le Mariquet and Hérouvillette, with the 1st Special Service Brigade under their orders on the high ground of Le Plein and near the little village of Bréville, soon to become the scene of a fierce battle. The fighting during those forty-eight hours had gained for the Division all its objectives with the exception of a small coastal strip near Franceville. They had suffered 800 casualties and more than 1,000 parachutists had not yet reached their rendezvous.

It was hoped and intended very soon to relieve them by troops coming in from the sea, but for various reasons this hope dwindled and then faded. The days passed and then the weeks and then the months and still the Division fought on. It was a battle of defence against very heavy pressure from the best formations which Rommel and his successor, Von Kluge, could throw against them. To describe it in detail is not possible within the compass of a short account; but one battle, the capture and retention of the village of Bréville, is of special importance, not merely as an illustration of the kind of warfare which the Division was called upon to wage in Normandy, but because defeat at that moment might have had the most serious consequences.

The days immediately following the landing were spent by the Division in consolidating its position, beating off counter-attacks and welcoming the arrival of small, scattered bodies of parachute troops, who gradually made their way, marching like good soldiers, to the sound of the guns. Their adventures had been many. Here are two. A parachute soldier landed in the garden of an enemy headquarters in Hérouvillette and, hearing a quiet call of 'Tommy,' flung a grenade in the direction of the voice, fortunately without effect, for the speaker was a member of the Forces Francaises de I'Interieure and guided him to safety. Then there was the GSO1 of the Division, who landed among mines at Varaville and fought all day with 'a surprising number of snipers.' During one of these engagements his steel helmet was struck so violently by a fragment of mortar bomb that the dent caused knocked it out of shape and made it impossible to wear, though the officer escaped with a scalp wound. Brigadier Poett's account of the actions of his, brigade paints a picture of resolute and controlled fighting in which the battle swayed now to one side, now to the other, among villages of yellow-grey stone with the lovely names of Herouvillette, Longueval and Ste-Honorine.

'Distributed amongst the brigade positions we had some forty anti-tank guns. I was therefore praying for a German counter-attack. My prayers were answered on June 8th. Preceded by heavy concentrations from mortars and SP guns, the counter-attack developed from Ste-Honorine towards Le Bas de Ranville, but only in a disappointingly small way as regards the numbers of tanks that disclosed themselves. Only three Tiger tanks and one armoured car were actually located, but others were undoubtedly firing from concealed positions. The counter-attack was decisively defeated, although some infiltration by infantry continued for a time.'

The Germans did not take very long to recover from the surprise of the airborne landings and their counter-attacks soon developed in force. For three days the battle raged in or near the small village of Bréville, near the high ground of Le Plein which had been so desperately held against the assaults of the 9th Parachute Battalion on the morning of the invasion.

There was no doubt that the enemy, who had succeeded in holding the village, was seeking to make a determined thrust from it towards the coast. If successful, he would cut the Airborne Division in half and be in a position to threaten the left flank of the whole British Army. A small gap had indeed already been made and very heavy casualties caused to the Special Service Brigade and the 12th Parachute Battalion. The enemy was determined to widen this gap if he could and by the evening of the 10th he had almost succeeded. On the next day the 51st Division, with bitter memories of St. Valery in their hearts, made a resolute attempt to drive back the Germans and close the gap. Their leading regiment, a battalion of the Black Watch, suffered very heavily and gained nothing by its resolution. Brigadier Hill, hastily mustering all the men he could, mostly tough Canadian parachute soldiers in action for the first time, led a counter-attack which temporarily restored the situation. The position, however, was very grave, almost desperate; Gale, the Divisional Commander, realized that the Brigade was in no position to withstand another attack. He realized also that the enemy was in bad shape and had lost at least as many men as the defence. The exhaustion on both sides was very great, but which was the more exhausted? Gale believed that it was the enemy and therefore determined, despite the very few troops at his disposal, to launch one more attack at the moment when the summer dusk deepened into night. His only reserve was the gallant 12th Parachute Battalion, now but 300 strong and 'B' Company of the 12th Battalion of the Devonshire Regiment. He had also a squadron of Sherman tanks and all the available artillery in the neighbourhood, which comprised five field and one medium regiment.

'Without orders we dug our slit trenches. Little did we know it during our previous training, but these trenches were to play a very important part in our life during the days ahead in Europe. They would afford vital protection, but would for long periods be our homes, where we would eat, sleep, wash, shave, write letters, in fact do practically everything. Unfortunately they were not weatherproof and when the heavy rain came, you just sat with a wet backside and hoped that the incessant drip-drip would stop soon and mostly it did. In the morning you dried out the best you could and hoped that you'd find a better hole next night.'
R. G. Lloyd, 12th Parachute Battalion.

'We were dropped at about 600 feet a few miles inland. As I left the aircraft, I could see some light flak coming up slowly, it seemed like long strings of flaming sausages and fires were burning inland, probably part of the work of Allied bombing. After landing safely in open country, my first impression was not what I'd expected. It was very quiet, considering. After releasing myself from my 'chute and retrieving my kitbag which contained a small radio set, I commenced my steady walk towards what I thought should be our rendezvous. But to my dismay my feet became entangled in what I took to be broken telephone wires. What a horrible twanging noise they made and I felt sure that being so loud, must be heard by the enemy, but of course this was all exaggerated due to my being keyed up. I found a crossroads and a few of my comrades.'

W. G. Lloyd of Ipswich, 12th Parachute Battalion.

The 12th Parachute Battalion, which had been resting all day, was ordered to make ready that evening. The men were concentrated in the church at Amfreville, where they waited until ten pm. Then they left the church, formed up outside and whiled away another five minutes reading copies of Pegasus, - the Divisional newspaper, handed out to them by the chaplain. The order came to advance and they went forward, following a wall of smoke and flame and noise. Some of the houses in the village began to burn so brightly that dusk was turned into the semblance of a red dawn.

The fight was short but very fierce, for the airborne troops would be content with nothing but victory. 'B' Company, rising from a field of clover, reached the edge of the village, killed a number of Germans in slit trenches and then went through between the burning houses to an orchard on the other side, where they dug in and held on. 'C' Company attacked on the left and lost their reserve platoon by shellfire before they started. They reached a hedge held by the enemy and sought to use the bayonet, but the Germans would not stay for them and fled. The Devons were less fortunate. They suffered very heavy casualties during the time spent in forming up for the attack and only a few of them reached the village.

At one moment, soon after the loss of Lieutenant-Colonel A. P. Johnston DSO commanding the 12th Parachute Battalion, the position was critical. It was saved by Colonel R. G. Parker DSO, Deputy Commander of the 6th Air Landing Brigade who, although himself wounded in the hand, assumed command and set by his leadership an example which 'was a big factor in the success' of the battalion. The enemy's guns were tackled and silenced by the Sherman tanks and within an hour the village was taken and the gap closed. The news of victory was brought to Brigadiers Lord Lovat and the Hon. A. K. M. Kindersley CBE as they lay badly wounded in the aid post. That night the airborne troops ranged through the burning village dealing with snipers, one of whom was found lying dead in bed with, above his head, a notice written in English pinned to the wall with his knife, 'Even if we fight alone, England must fall.'

For the remainder of the month of June, for all July and for the first fortnight of August, the Division held the line, suffering casualties, notably in the fighting round Le Mesnil, but each time giving much more than they received. Then at last, on 17 August, the order for a general advance came and in ten days the airborne troops, now reinforced with some stout Dutch and Belgian regiments, swept forward up to the outskirts of Le Havre. So rapid and pertinacious were they, that the enemy had no chance to stand and fight, despite the nature of the country, which is well wooded and cut up by streams and rivers, the chief being the Touges. Gale gave them no rest, moving his brigades in a series of leapfrogs and delivering his attacks both by day and night. The first main action was fought at Putot en Auge, which was captured during a night attack by the 7th, 12th and 13th Parachute Battalions on August 19th, when 'the fighting spirit of the troops was beyond all praise.' They had had no sleep for forty-eight hours, yet throughout the day their dash and energy never diminished and in the evening they were in tremendous heart.

Next came the fight for Pont L 'Eveque, Here the crossing of the rivet was 'to be forced immediately at all costs,' so as to leave the enemy no time to consolidate. The assault took place under cover of smoke and proved a hard task. A few men got over the river near a ford and a larger number by means of a broken railway bridge. A troop of tanks was held up, but an armoured bulldozer succeeded in pushing sufficient debris from the burning houses of Pont L 'Eveque into the stream and the tanks were able to reach the other side. At one moment the gallant 13th Battalion had to withdraw from their small bridgehead and despite every effort during two days and a night of hard fighting it proved impossible to eject the enemy. His casualties, however, had been so severe that on the night of August 23rd / 24th he slipped away. There was finally the capture of Pont Audemer, which was accomplished on August 26th.

As mile after mile of this advance from the Orne and the Dives was covered and the sun of victory shone ever brighter and brighter; the men forgot their fatigue, forgot that they had been holding the line as ordinary infantry; and realized only that they were the victors, 'I regard this march as definitely one of the outstanding feats of the battalion,' writes a Commanding Officer. 'It was expected that men would fall out with foot trouble; ambulances were, in fact, following up to lift such cases. The battalion, as stated, led the column and marched at light infantry pace, rapidly drawing farther and farther ahead. Not a single man fell out.'

The leading elements of the Devons, who had reached Touges on August 24th, commandeered a fire engine and a milk float and in these set out for Honfleur. Being run on coal gas, neither vehicle could surmount the hills. The first was driven by a fireman wearing a brass helmet, the second by its owner, the milkman; they took the leading platoon, somewhat hampered by the presence of an interpreter whose knowledge of English was less than theirs of French, to within a mile and a half of the town. Thence the Devons went forward on foot and presently found themselves in its main square surrounded by cheering men and women, of whom many were armed with rifles. These went off at frequent intervals until 'we explained to them the use of the safety catch.'

The enemy was still in the town and there was much sniping, but this did not deter the eager citizens from greeting with an almost embarrassing enthusiasm Allies who had marched so far and accomplished so much. 'We had a warm welcome from the mademoiselles,' reported Private Rawson 'and a greengrocer opened his entire shop for us.' The citizens rejoiced and the sound of their cheering echoed all over Europe. There for a moment we can leave the gallant 6th Airborne. They had done more than win their spurs; they had taken part in the most remarkable of all the invasions which the Continent of Europe has had to endure. It was an invasion not of savages thirsty for loot and women and conquest, but of liberators come to undo the deeds of savages whom to describe as Huns is to insult the followers of Attila. The men of the 6th Airborne Division were in advance of the van. That must always be their pride and their reward.'

D-DAY: *The Sixth Airborne Prepares.*

Red Devils' Timeline

The 6th Airborne Division is to support Sir Miles Dempsey's British Second Army and Henry Crerar's First Canadian Army. 6th Airborne's task is to seize and hold the left flank of the bridgehead. Brigadier Poett's 5th Parachute Brigade is to seize the ground each side of the bridges over the Canal du Caen and the Orne River and on the same day seize and hold positions on the long wooded ridge beyond the waterways, running from Troarn in the south to the sea. This ridge with the bridges behind will eventually form the critical left flank of the army and the bridges have to be intact to permit Allied troops and supplies to pass easily to and fro.

Brigadier James Hill's 3rd Parachute Brigade, made up of the 8th and 9th Battalions and the 1st Canadian Parachute Battalion (1,800 men) is to prevent enemy reinforcements moving towards the British beachhead. The 8th Battalion and the 1st Canadian Brigade are to destroy five bridges in the flooded valley of the Dives. The 9th Battalion, commanded by Lieutenant Colonel Terence B. H. Otway DSO is to silence a battery of four concrete gun emplacements on high ground near the village of Merville, 3 miles east of Ouistreham.

5 June
38 and 46 Groups RAF dispatch 264 aircraft and 98 glider combinations, the glider tugs being Albemarles, Dakotas, Halifaxes and Stirlings, the gliders mainly Horsas with a few Hamilcars (carrying light tanks and 17-pounder anti-tank guns).
2230   Coup de main party takes off from Tarrant Rushton, Dorset in six Horsa gliders towed by Halifax bombers of 298 and 644 Squadrons, who will bomb Caen after the gliders are released.
2249   Seven Horsas leave Down Ampney behind Dakotas of 271 Squadron.
2250   Dakotas of 233 Squadron tow six Horsas into the air above Blakehill Farm.
2310   Four Horsas carrying paratroops and medical staff leave Harwell towed by Albemarles of 295 and 570 Squadrons.

6 June
0015   At 5,000 feet over Cabourg the gliders carrying the coup de main party are released from their tugs and they begin their five-mile glide to the bridges over the Canal de Caen and Orne River.
0020   Three of the gliders land within 30 yards of the Canal de Caen bridge.
0020   North of Ranville pathfinders with radar beacons and coloured lights to mark the dropping zones, together with the advance parties if the 5th Parachute Brigade, drop from 27 aircraft.

0035 Canal de Caen bridge (subsequently renamed 'Pegasus Bridge') is in British hands at a cost of two men killed and 14 wounded. Two other gliders land near the Orne River bridge (subsequently renamed 'Horsa Bridge'), which is undefended. (A sixth glider lands seven miles away near the Dives River). Howard has to beat off counter-attacks from German tanks and artillery for more than 12 hours. Spitfires fly over at about 10,000 feet and Howard signals that they have captured the bridge. His men watch as they do victory rolls and one drops a package of the morning papers. 'Howard says, 'Right then my blokes forgot about the bridge and the war. They were riveted by the *Daily Mirror* and the sight of *Jane* taking her skirt off.'

0050 2,000 men of the 5th Parachute Brigade and 400 containers dropped north of Ranville by 110 RAF aircraft.

0230 Main Force of 750 men of the 9th Battalion attacking the Merville battery leaves Brize Norton, Harwell and Tarrant Rushton in Horsas towed by Albemarles.

0030-0040 Low cloud obscures the Merville battery. Out of a total force of 104 aircraft, 83 Halifaxes and ten Lancasters of 6 Group attack at 00.25 hours. Three of the five Mosquitoes dispatched are able to release their markers, which are rather scattered and appear as indistinct glows beneath the cloud. Nearly all the 4,000lb bombs dropped miss the target. Gonneville-en-Auge, a small hamlet immediately to the south of the battery, is reported to be mistaken for the German battery and the village is heavily bombed.

0250 9th Battalion paratroop drops are scattered and only about 150 paras are grouped together for the march on the Battery.

0300 7th Battalion, 5th Brigade, cross the Orne Bridge, take up positions in Bénouville and Le Port and for the rest of the day fight off a series of attacks by elements of the German 716th Division.

0330 60 tugs cast off their gliders, which land on dropping zones to disgorge General 'Windy' Gale and his Divisional HQ and the anti-tank batteries with their six-pounder guns.

0445 Merville Battery surrenders.

1250 As the Germans move to counter-attack the 5th Parachute Brigade lands and its 7th Battalion moves to reinforce the defensive positions around the bridges.

1330 Brigadier Lord Lovat's 1st Special Service Brigade composed of four Army, and one Royal Marines Commando, reach Pegasus Bridge en route to help other units of the Airborne Division.

1500 7th Battalion occupies Bénouville and Le Port, the villages closest to the bridges and holds them against repeated counter-attacks by 21st Panzer. Madame Vion, whose 18th Century château was being used as a shelter for unmarried mothers, provided British paratroopers with baths and drinking water. She had successfully resisted German attempts to take over her home.

2051-2123. Operation Mallard. There are insufficient aircraft to carry the 6th Airborne Division in one lift so 256 Dakota, Albemarle, Stirling and Halifax tugs of 38 and 46 Groups towing 30 Hamilcar and 226 Horsa gliders, escorted by 15 RAF fighter squadrons, transport most of Brigadier Kindersley's 6th

Air Landing Brigade equipped with Tetrarch light tanks, Bren-gun carriers, 25-pounder field guns, scout cars and even Bailey bridge pontoons and one regiment of artillery of three batteries armed with American 75 mm pack howitzers. In all, 249 gliders land on their landing zones behind 'Utah' and east of the Orne. One Horsa crashes on take-off three break their tows en route and three are forced to ditch in the Channel. A further 50 Dakotas undertake supply-dropping sorties with 116 tons of ammunition, food and equipment in Operation 'Rob Roy'. As the Dakotas approach low from seawards on their supply mission they are mistaken for a further wave of German bombers that had just attacked the shipping. Heavy anti-aircraft fire causes the formation to scatter, forcing some aircraft to return damaged. One ditches in the Channel and five others are missing. Less than a quarter of the supplies are delivered.

In all, Nine Dakotas, two Albemarles, one Halifax and a Stirling are lost. The Glider Pilot Regiment loses 34 pilots killed in action on D-Day.

'As a glider pilot, my objective was a small corner of a particularly tiny field of rough pasture close to the Orne Bridge. If I overshot, I would crush us all against a 14-foot high embankment - if I undershot I would destroy my seven tons of powerless aircraft and its human cargo on a belt of 50-foot-high trees. There was simply no room for error. The significance of the two bridges to be attacked by a coup de main force was emphasised to us. With the 6th Airborne Division landing to the east of the river and the whole invasion coming ashore to the west of the canal, it was vital that these troops should be able to cross the two bridges over the Orne and the canal. These two bridges were the only ones where you could do this between Caen and the sea. So it was absolutely vital that we had the maximum surprise element and the only way to do this was for us to carry out our operation before the rest of the invasion started. So we were going to sneak in just after midnight and some six-and-a-half hours before the seaborne invasion came ashore. Someone had made a most marvellous sand-table, a perfect model of what was on the ground in Normandy - even down to the last tree and ditch. The chap who'd made it had put some wires above the area and slid a cine camera down these wires, filming all the way and therefore had simulated what a glider pilot would see on his approach. It was incredibly clever and impressed us all very much. So we were very confident. Each Horsa glider with its 88-foot wingspan was going to carry 28 troops, a mixture of Ox and Bucks Light Infantry, plus two or three Engineers - we were also going to carry an assault boat and numerous other bits of equipment, because it was thought that the bridges might be blown before we got there. We got out on to the airfield about 21:30 on 5 June. I think everyone knew on the airfield what was happening except one of the ground staff from the Air Force, who came up to me and said, 'Are you bringing this one back tonight, Staff?' I said, 'No. I don't think so.' He walked away looking dazed.

'We'd met the Ox and Bucks lads a few days before and they were a very good bunch. However, on the night they arrived all blacked up, loaded with arms and ammunition, they looked a right bunch of cut-throats - I think I was more afraid of them than I was of the Germans. We loaded up, drank a cup of tea, chatted and at about twenty to eleven, when it was nearly dark-we had double summertime in those days - we mounted up and when somebody fired the green flare, the engines started and one by one we got under way.'

Staff Sergeant Roy Howard, Glider Pilot Regiment, who landed East of the canal at the Orne bridge was the only glider to find the landing zone. Howard skidded through a herd of terrified cows to bring his Horsa within 20 feet of his objective. A second glider was down intact a couple of fields away and the third had mistaken a bridge on the Dives River, 10 miles away, for the objective.

'I felt this bang in my wrist and that was it. The next thing I remember was being in this house on the floor with my arm in a sling across my chest. My right arm was pretty mucky. Because I had lost a lot of blood, I was terribly thirsty all the time. The next thing I remember is lying on the beach, under this tarpaulin cover. Then we were put on a DUKW and taken out to a tank landing ship. The doctor had got a sort of emergency theatre. He redressed my arm, which by this time had begun to smell a bit because gangrene had set in. After a while, I felt wet and uncomfortable, so I called a nurse and she turned the bedclothes back and there was all blood everywhere. I had haemorrhaged, she left the clothes turned back and rushed off to get the sister. I looked down and instead of my arm across my chest as I thought, there was nothing there. My arm had gone, which was a bit shattering.'

Staff Sergeant Geoffrey Barkway, glider pilot, 2nd Battalion, Glider Pilot Regiment.

'We lived in the lower area of Bréville. At this time there were bombing raids on Merville where there were German gun batteries to cover the beaches.[3] On 4 June we were forced to leave our home. My father feared for our safety as there was a central communications blockhouse just 300 metres from the house which had not yet been bombed and he took us to the Château-Ste-Côme where we moved into some unused horse stalls.[4] The château itself was occupied by the Germans, just as the important houses and places like 'le Belvedere' in Bréville were. Except for the intense bombing of Merville, we never suffered. On the other hand, the night of 5 June became a night of enormous and continuous noise. My father and other adults went out into

3   On the night of 19/20 May 63 aircraft - 42 Halifaxes, 15 Lancasters and six Mosquitoes of 6 and 8 Groups bombed the gun position at Merville. Some bombs did fall in the battery position despite the presence of haze. A direct hit in the Mairie, used as the officers' mess killed 18 including Hauptmann Karl-Heinrich Wolter, the battery commander, and his French girl friend.
4   This fine example of a small chateau had once been a famous facing stud where some of the finest French racing stock was bred. Now the stables had been reduced to rubble and many of the horses killed.

the night. A glider had landed in a hedgerow just 200 metres away. My father and his friends hid the seriously wounded pilot on an embankment and women cared for him and took him food. The next morning he had disappeared. Later, we saw English soldiers with blackened faces and branches on their helmets passing the livestock outbuildings. They had an odd effect on me. We also saw German patrols that were being directed from the château. The advanced German lines were between Bréville and Gonneville where there was lots of weaponry - cannons and all sorts of materials.'

7½ years old Jacques Courcy. 'On 6 June, we, the kids, remained hidden in the livestock outbuildings of the château while my father went to find food for everyone. He didn't return until the night of 6/7 June because of the battle taking place. On 7 June an English patrol commanded by Lieutenant Christie of the 9th Para came and asked my father if he had seen a glider land near to the castle. Father took them to the place where two gliders had landed. However, the English paratroopers were caught by a German patrol that was passing on bicycles, but fortunately suffered no harm. At the entrance to Bréville, in a small wood, there was a German gun battery that overlooked the Château-Ste-Côme. The English Commandos [sic] took this assault battery during the attack on Bréville-les-Monts. The château was hit by an artillery shell and was alternatively occupied during the attacks and counter-attacks. After each attack, the English returned to Amfreville. Every day my father went out to look for eggs, milk and other things to eat or to help the English soldiers. Twenty of us remained in the livestock outbuildings until the 12th or 13th of June and returned to our house at the end of August. It was a wreck. The walls and windows had taken many artillery rounds and the wardrobe doors had been used to cover the trenches.' [5]

'Just before midnight Sunday 4 June I was lying on a gas cape spread over wet ground inside a bivouac made of groundsheets on the perimeter of Keevil airfield going over coming events. The 6th Airborne Division was to spearhead the invasion of Europe and secure the left flank of the Landing Beaches. The next day was spent resting during the morning, a short service after lunch and then a final check of personal equipment. Together with spare clothes I had 100 rounds .303 (50 tracer and 50 incendiary), 4 x No.36 grenades fitted with 4 second fuses, anti tank Gammon Bombs and four spare Bren gun mags, a Lee Enfield rifle and a telescopic sight (I was a sniper). In addition I had to carry an inflatable rubber dinghy attached to

5   By 10 June the village was still in enemy hands. On 11 June the paras, reinforced by the Black Watch, carried out another assault but it failed. The Black Watch, in their first battle, suffered 200 casualties. Next day the 12th Parachute Regiment, the 12th Devons and the tanks of the 13th/18th Hussars assaulted through the 1 Commando Brigade positions from the direction of Amfreville and took the village. A total of 141 paratroopers of the 160 who took part in the assault became casualties; the Germans losing 418 out of their 564 men. Afterwards, the 12th Devons took over positions in the grounds of the Château-Ste-Côme.

my right leg (to cross any water obstacles if the Ox & Bucks failed to capture the bridges). Loading into an adapted Stirling bomber I learned that the aircraft was to go on a dummy bombing raid prior to dropping us. I found my place in the line of 20 paras, which the aircraft carried. We all sat on the floor; even numbers on one side and odd numbers on the other. No smoking until we were airborne so to ease the tension we sang paras songs to the tune of *'Knees up Mother Brown'*, the end of the chorus going, *'I'll always keep my trousers on when jumping through the hole'*. I wondered if that would be true that night.

'We took off and as we neared the French coast anti-aircraft shells started bursting all around the plane causing it to rock, but the pilot flew straight towards our target area near the village of Ranville. Suddenly, a red light appeared near the rear of the aircraft, which denoted 20 seconds to the commencement of the drop. The tension could have been cut with a knife; we were all as taut as bow-strings. Soon the voice of the dispatcher was heard, 'Stand up, Hook up'. We formed a single line down the centre of the aircraft and each man hooked up the man in front of him. The Despatcher opened the floor doors and remarked, 'There are thousands of ships down there so you'll soon have plenty of company. The red light changed to green and the dispatcher shouted, 'GO'.

'The first man disappeared through the hole in the floor, swiftly followed by others who were shuffling towards it, until it was my turn at No.17. I stepped into space, but just as I did so the plane rocked and I hit both sides of the hole during my exit, breaking my army watch which I later found had stopped at 0036 hours.

'I heard the crack of the chute developing slowing my descent. I grabbed the rope holding the kit bag on my leg and pulled the quick release, then lowered it to its full length. I had a quick look round, noting the pretty patterns made by the searchlights and tracer bullets. Many searchlights were trying to locate our planes whilst the tracer shells and bullets weaved a beautiful pattern in the night sky. Then in the distance I saw a church with a detached tower, silhouetted against the lighted background, which I instantly recognised as Ranville Church. I had seen it many times before on photographs and the scale model of the dropping area. I heard a thump as my kitbag hit the ground. Then for a full minute, I was violently sick from the fear and the release of tension.

'Stand with your back to the church and run forward and slightly left, there you will find a road leading to the bridges' These words were imprinted in my brain and I blindly followed instructions. Gathering my kitbag I turned my back towards Ranville Church and ran. I knew I would find the road that led to the bridges now known at Horsa and Pegasus bridges. I shuffled on under my heavy load and then the W/Op shouted 'Ham and Jam', the signal that the bridges had been captured intact by the Ox & Bucks bridge party. I immediately discarded the kit bag, as the dinghy would no longer be needed. Soon we had made a group of 20 to 30 parachutists, one of whom was a wireless operator, who was trying to make contact with the bridge party. Had they captured the bridges intact?

'We were about 200 yards from the first bridge when the wireless operator signalled the glider troops had captured the bridges intact. We raced onwards and as we approached the Canal de Caen Bridge I saw a number of dead bodies amongst whom was an officer, lying in the roadway. On the other side of the bridge there appeared to be a mighty battle in progress but this turned out to be ammunition exploding in a German tank that had been destroyed by the Glider Troops. We made our way through Bénouville but near the château gates we made contact with the enemy. Private McCara climbed over a hedge and was knifed to death by two Germans waiting on the other side. A No.36 hand grenade with a four seconds fuse was thrown over the hedge into the slit trench that the Germans had then occupied. A machine gun then opened fire from inside the château gates wounding Private Whittingham who later died of his wounds. A German stick grenade exploded near the head of our officer who started to bleed from his eyes and ears, which gave us the impression that he had a fractured base of the skull. So we withdrew, taking our wounded with us.

'We set up a defensive position astride the main Caen-Ouistreham road on a bank of earth bordering a sunken cart track that was about 10 feet wide. On the opposite side of the track and immediately in front of us was a seven-foot brick wall with a wooden door at one end. We were now on the seaward side of Bénouville. Our position enabled us to control any enemy movement along the main Caen-Ouistreham road as well as preventing him from making any attack on the bridges from the western side of the village. The night was taken up with small patrol skirmishes.

Order Of Battle
6th Airborne Division
Major General Richard Gale

3rd Parachute Brigade
8th and 9th Battalions, The Parachute Regiment, AAC
1st Canadian Parachute Battalion

5th Parachute Brigade
7th, 12th and 13th Battalions, The Parachute Regiment, AAC

6th Airlanding Brigade
2nd Battalion The Oxfordshire and Buckinghamshire Light Infantry
1st Battalion The Royal Ulster Rifles
'A' Company 12th Battalion The Devonshire Regiment

Divisional Troops
HQ 6th Airborne Division
6th Airborne Armoured Reconnaissance Regt, RAG

211 Battery, 53rd Airlanding Light Regiment, Royal Artillery
3rd and 4th Airlanding Anti-Tank Batteries, Royal Artillery
3rd and 591st Parachute Squadrons, Royal Engineers
249th Field Company (Airborne), Royal Engineers
286th Field Park Company (Airborne), Royal Engineers
22nd Independent Parachute Company
1st and 2nd Wings Glider Pilot Regiment, AAC

Plus Airborne elements of:
Royal Corps of Signals
Royal Army Service Corps
Royal Army Medical Corps
Corps of Royal Electrical and Mechanical Engineers

'By morning we were completely surrounded but we had to hang on until relieved by the commandos. The Germans launched several counter attacks, one of which penetrated to the far side of a wall about ten feet in front of me. I knocked a stick grenade which landed close to me into a sunken lane in front of me and I replied with one of my grenades, which silenced things a lot. At about 1030 three large Panther tanks, came rumbling along the main road from the direction of Caen. They stopped near the château gates and the one to my right opened fire. The shell hit a wall about three or four yards to my left. Private McGee, who was near the main road, picked up his Bren gun then started to walk up the middle of the road towards the tanks firing the Bren gun from his hip. As one magazine became empty, he replaced it with a new one, discarding the empty magazine on the roadside. We could hear the bullets ricocheting off the armour steel plating of the leading tank that immediately closed down his visor, thus making him blind to things in front! Corporal Tommy Killeen realised what was happening and ran up the side of the road, taking two Gammon bombs from his pouches. He threw the first bomb which hit the leading tank where the turret and body meets which nearly blew the turret off. He threw the second bomb but being further away from the second tank, it fell short, landing against the tank's track, which was promptly blown off. This tank now tried to escape, but only having one good track it went around in circles, so the crew bailed out and tried to escape. They were shot by McGee.

Just after midday I heard the sound of the bagpipes coming from the direction of Ste-Aubin and knew that Lord Lovat's commandos had made it and we were no longer alone. About 2130 the 2nd Warwicks attacked Bénouville and relieved us with the remainder of my company. I made my way back to the bridge where I had my first meal that day. About 0100 on 7 June I made my way back to the Dropping Zone where I dug a hole 7 feet long, 2 feet wide and 2 feet deep, lined it with part of a discarded chute, covered myself with the other part and fell asleep. It certainly had been a very long day.

Sergeant Edgar 'Eddie' Gurney BEM, 7th (LI) Battalion, 5th Parachute Brigade, who also recalls:
'Our dead were buried later in Ranville churchyard. One of them is 19-year old Emil Courteil who was more or less pressed into being a dog handler because he had been caught poaching in England, or so the story goes. When he was put on a charge and brought before the commanding officer he was told that he would be given a lighter sentence if he volunteered to be a dog handler. He did. Unfortunately, he and dog and others in his aircraft were dropped astray and they were trying to get make their way back to the Merville battery when they saw a quantity of aircraft coming in quite low. When they got nearer they recognised the aircraft as British and they waved to them. Unfortunately Emil and the others were in the wrong place and the RAF had instructions to machine gun anything that moved in that area and Emile and his dog 'Glen' with other members of the 9th Parachute Battalion, were killed. The inscription on Emil's headstone reads:

'Had you known our boy you would have loved him too. 'Glen' his paratroop dog was killed with him.'[6]

'It was just growing dusk on the 5th June when we got in the Stirling four engine jobs. We were all very quiet. The RAF came round with canisters of tea, but nobody wanted any! As we went over the Channel and over France I held my breath - the world seemed to stand still - THIS WAS IT - the start of everything, I thought of my wife at home, I hoped I would come through and I prayed to God, as many others did and as I did at Dunkirk. He must have been listening to me and perhaps thought I still wasn't good enough to die! When we approached the Dropping Zone the plane was getting hit, it was like driving on a new road with the grit hitting the body work - it was only light stuff, but it still sounded fearful!

'The Red Light came on and then the Green Light - this was the moment - we all had to jump through the hole in the floor. I had a kit-bag and Bren etc. It took one or two seconds to get through as there were more men with kit-bags and equipment and the plane was going like hell. I think the pilot had his foot through the headlights!

'I landed awkwardly with the kit-bag tope wrapped round my boot, I thought I had broken my foot and I had wrenched my arm badly, I could still feel the heat of the plane's engine and I still can! I also thought about the cups of tea we had turned down in the aircraft! I could still use my toes so I went to a pre-arranged point two or three miles away. When I reached our rendezvous we found Jerry giving us heavy fire from his armoured cars. My companion was hit when we came across three or four Germans. I fired my Colt revolver to stop them following me. We were near a church and suddenly all hell broke loose. A Jerry started to machine gun us. We did a flanking movement and went round behind him. Then the lads went in with

---

6   The Alsatian, usually keen to jump from aircraft, seemed hesitant on D-Day but they made it safely to the ground. When they were found, 'Glen' was still linked to his master by his lead. They were buried together. Bing, a second dog, which also descended in a tailor-made parachute, dropped into Normandy with the paras. The Alsatian had to be rescued from a tall tree that had snagged the dog's canopy. The paras found Bing useful because he heard enemy gunfire and vehicles well before they did and he was able to guide his handler, Ken Bailey, through enemy lines following the landing. Bing received the 'animal VC,' the Dickin Medal of the People's Dispensary for Sick Animals. He was returned to his owner after the war. See: D-Day: The Greatest Invasion - A People's History by Dan Van Der Vat (Madison Press Books Toronto 2003). Ranville War Cemetery contains 2,562 burials including 2,151 British, 322 German and 76 Canadian. Nearly all died on 6/7 June 1944. Among those buried there are the brother Lieutenants Maurice and Philippe Rousseau from Montreal, Canada. Maurice, the elder brother, arrived in Britain in 1941 and ten months before D-Day, married a girl from Preston. Philippe landed in France with the 1st Canadian Parachute Battalion on the 6 June and was killed the following day. Typhoon pilot, Squadron Leader J. R. Collins DFC* was KIA over Ranville on 11 August when his parachute failed to open. Glasgow army padre, Robert Cape, attached to the Black Watch, was killed on 25 June. 16 year-old Private Robert Johns from Portsmouth was killed on 23 July while serving with the Parachute Regiment. Lance Corporal Peter Moody, whose real name was Kurt Meyer, a young Jewish soldier of German extraction, in 10 Inter-Allied Commando, was killed on 13 June. In the adjoining churchyard, a further 47 British soldiers including Lieutenant Den Brotheridge, are buried close to the perimeter wall. A Guide to the Beaches and Battlefields of Normandy by David Evans (Michael Joseph, 1995 and Amberley 2010).

the steel. That finished that problem. After forming up we started to move to our objective: Bréville. Its capture was essential - it was to be done at all costs. It was on high ground overlooking a valley through which the Germans could percolate at any time into the bridgehead which was to be established unless we took it.

'We formed up in an area only 3/4-mile from Bréville and came under terrific mortar pounding from the Germans. As darkness fell our artillery opened up in support of us and soon the night was lit up by tracer and the deafening din of artillery from the Allied lines and counter fire from the German mortars. As we stormed up towards the village one after another of our men fell on the way, but we went on, determined to do the job we had been given. Despite the killed and wounded we eventually fought our way into Bréville where the battle raged on at dose quarters until Jerry was driven out.

'Then we started our next job with no respite - digging in frenziedly to await the inevitable counter attack from the mortars! We were not disappointed. Within a quarter-of-an-hour the inferno began and the entire village seemed to be ablaze. The Germans knew its importance as much as we did! But we clung on, despite everything. At the height of the bombardment we lost the sergeant-major and our colonel. The colonel was dashing about rallying everyone and shouting 'Dig in you .... or die.' Shortly afterwards he was killed - and many of our lads and my comrades DID die. One lad was lucky - he had his helmet blown open just like a tin can - he was wounded, but he was lucky to be even alive after a hit like that. He was distressed and yelling. I put him on a jeep and carried him out then went back to pick up the others.

'Throughout the long night we waited for the German counterattack against what was now a shambles of a village - not with mortars now - but with infantry. It never came. Not until prisoners were interrogated later did we learn that we had given them such a hammering that they had neither the strength nor the will to make another effort. But we didn't know that at the time and so through the next day and night we stuck it out and after two days, VERY tired and weary, we were relieved. Incidentally I carried out the lad who had his helmet blown off and took him to a jeep to get him out of the line of fire. But when I got to it I found the rear tyre was ablaze and I had to put it out by smothering it with horse or cow manure.

'Things were too hectic for me to take much notice which it was! It was at this time that I realised I had been wounded in the leg. I hadn't had time to notice until then!

'By this time the church and everything else was on fire. Shells from our own artillery were hitting us as well because apparently the Officer directing the shelling had been killed and so we got both lots: British artillery and German mortars!

'When we were relieved I was taken to the Royal Navy and so back to England where my report from the hospital at Blackpool gave my problem as 'leg wound and exhaustion'.

'One incident that shows how fate plays a part: one of my mates dropped his fighting knife just before we set off and cut his foot. We dressed it for him and said nothing because he didn't want to be left behind. But he had trouble in walking once we got there and so he was left to look after the equipment when the shelling started. He was promptly hit by shellfire in the lower head and neck.

'When General, later Field Marshal, Montgomery held a Field investiture for officers and men of the Airborne Division, one DSO went to the Colonel and one MC and two DCMs and four Military Medals to other officers and men of the 12th Yorkshire Parachute Battalion. Only one was present at the investiture to collect his award - the rest was either killed or wounded. That about says what it was all about.'

Charles Pearson 12th Yorkshire Parachute Battalion (AAC) Independent section, 5th Parachute Brigade

'My brigade task was to seize, intact, the bridges over the River Orne and the Canal de Caen at Bénouville and Ranville and establish a bridgehead. As my small aircraft skimmed over the defences of the Atlantic Wall, not a shot was fired. The red light came on and then the green. I was 'out', seconds later a bump. It was the soil of France. The time some 20 minutes after midnight on the 5/6 June 1944. The darkness was complete; the silence unbroken except for the sound of my disappearing aircraft. A few minutes later the sky to the west lit up - firing, explosions, all the sights and sounds of battle. It was John Howard's assault. He also had been timed to land at 20 minutes after midnight. Now I must get to the bridges as quickly as possible and be able, if need be, to adjust the Brigade plan. Would the bridges be in the hands of friend or foe? Intact or damaged? Indeed Howard's Company had achieved a splendid success. The bridges were in our hands, intact. All was well!'

Brigadier Nigel Poett, Commander 5th Parachute Brigade who dropped with the pathfinders east of the Orne.

'Once the chaps had gone, this was a dodgy time for a glider pilot. I leapt out of the glider and crawled to the nearest ditch. There I threw off my flying helmet and equipment and proceeded to kit myself out as a soldier. It was a strange transition. We were trained soldiers, but we were also trained pilots, so our objective was a quick return to the UK for further flying, not to be involved with the fighting for longer than necessary. By the 8th June I was back at Tarrant Rushton, having been released by the operation commander at 2100 hours on D-Day.'

Staff Sergeant Roy Howard, Glider Pilot Regiment:
'We were literally staggering under the weight of the stuff we were carrying. I personally carried four fully loaded Bren-gun mags plus two bandoliers of .303 ammunition. I had six Mills 36 grenades, two 77 phosphorus smoke grenades, two Norwegian-type egg-shaped stun-grenades that just made a bang when you threw them. We carried a twenty-four-hour ration pack that consisted of cubes of tea, soup, oatmeal, toilet paper, sweets, matches and some fuel for our little Tommy cookers.

'The glider was twisting and turning a bit and, looking over the pilot's shoulder, you could see the bridge. It was exactly like the model we'd been shown but it suddenly vanished as the glider veered to make its approach to landing and the next thing - crash! - as it hit the deck. Sparks were flying left right and centre and all of a sudden it just came to a halt and there was silence again - just the creaking of timber in the glider. The undercarriage had gone and the front of the glider had caved in. Den Brotheridge, our platoon commander, quickly slid the door open and said, 'Gun Out!' which was me, so out I jumped and stumbled on the grass because of the weight I had on me. I set the Bren up facing the bridge and the rest of the lads jumped out. Den looked round to make sure that everyone was out and he said, 'Come on lads!' We were about thirty yards from the bridge and we dashed towards it. I saw a German on the right-hand side and I let rip at him and down he went. I still kept firing as I went over the bridge. On the other side was another German and he went down too.'

Private William Gray, 'D' Company, 2nd Battalion, Oxfordshire and Buckinghamshire Light Infantry.

'Our glider began dipping and the pilot was desperately pulling his control column back. He shouted to our platoon leader, Lieutenant Dennis Fox: 'Move two blokes from the front.' Two of the lads rushed to the back and our glider crash-landed at 90mph. Incredibly we got out unharmed. It was 00.19. We poured out towards the River Orne and the guards opened fire. We had expected resistance and I already had a two-inch mortar set up. My bombs landed on either side of the northern end of bridge and the guns fell silent. We stormed forward and found the Germans had scarpered. We were astonished to have taken the bridge so easily and two platoons were ordered to stand guard in case of a counter-attack. Meanwhile; Pegasus Bridge had been taken within ten minutes, but this time not without cost. Lieutenant Denny Brotheridge was the first Allied casualty of D-Day and two others were wounded.'

Sergeant 'Wagger' Thornton.

'I automatically looked at my watch; it had stopped at 0016 hours. As I experienced that never-to-be-forgotten moment, the leading section moved quietly up the small track leading to the bridge to their vital task of putting the pillbox out of action.

'I let Den Brotheridge and his platoon get out first because if they were indeed the first platoon down their job was absolutely one of speed. The leading section was to go up and put the pillbox out of action by throwing a smoke bomb on the road as they came up from the landing zone and through the smoke, throw short-fuse grenades through the gun slits of the pillbox and then continue with the rest of the platoon across the bridge. This had all been planned. Every platoon was ready to do that job in case they were the first platoon to get to the bridge that night.

'As I moved up myself I heard the dull thud of the phosphorous bomb and saw the greenish cloud of smoke which the section quickly dashed through to lob short-fuse HE grenades through the gun slits of the pillbox. 'In the meantime Den was moving up to the near end of the bridge with the rest of his platoon at his heels and as he and his men charged across the bridge we heard three or four ominous thuds inside the pillbox indicating that the grenades had done their stuff. I knew we'd get no trouble from there.

'Then the battle really started, enemy firing came from all directions but the first shots were from the direction of the Gondrée cafe, clearly aimed at Den and his platoon as they came off the far end of the bridge. Our chaps replied with gusto, no doubt running and firing guns from the hip. It was a tremendous sight to see all the tracer bullets firing in all directions. There seemed to be three different colours, red, yellow and white, with the enemy firing at us and my men firing at them as they went over the bridge. I simultaneously heard two more crashes which sounded like gliders pranging and I could hardly believe my ears. Within a very short time it seemed David Wood came steaming up from the landing zone with his platoon hard on his heels and I straightaway confirmed task No 2. As soon as he got into the trenches enemy firing started from several new directions. A runner came from the other side of the bridge with the sad news that Mr Brotheridge had been seriously hit in the neck during the opening burst of enemy firing as he came off the bridge and he was lying unconscious. I was just about to go over when Sandy Smith arrived with his platoon. He said his glider had had a very bad landing and there were several casualties. I then noticed that one of his arms was hanging limply and tucked into his battle-dress blouse. He was also limping badly. He assured me that he was fit enough to bash on so I confirmed No 3 task and as Den was out of action said he was to co-ordinate things on the other side of the bridge until I could arrange a relief. So off he went and skirmishing went on all round the bridge. Very soon after I learnt that David Wood, his Sergeant and radio operator had all run into enemy MG fire and were out of action the other side of the pillbox. They had apparently caught a German laying booby-trap mines in the trenches. I thus had only one of my three canal bridge platoon commanders on his feet and he had an injured arm and leg.

'Apart from the firing going on a great deal of noise emanated from platoons shouting code-names to identify friends in the dark and there was an unholy rabble of Able-Able-Able, Baker-Baker-Baker, Charlie-Charlie-Charlie and Sapper-Sapper-Sapper, coming from all directions; on top of automatic fire, tracer and the odd grenade it was hell let loose and most certainly would have helped any wavering enemy to make a quick decision about quitting.

'So I had three platoons down on the ground in exactly the same places where all the briefings had hoped they would be. But by this time I was suddenly wondering what was happening on the other bridge, which was only a quarter of a mile away and I couldn't see any signs of firing over there. There were no radio messages but that didn't surprise me because the radios in those days were pretty frail. I mean, in crash landings we didn't expect them to survive. But another part of my orders was that because of the radios being a bit uncertain a runner from each platoon would report to my company headquarters by the canal bridge, from the river bridge particularly, but no runners had arrived either. I was beginning to consider whether I would have to send a platoon or half a platoon over to the river bridge to try to capture that but then all the luck turned. The captain of the Royal Engineers, Captain Jock Neilson, reported to me that there were no explosives under the canal bridge: we found the explosives in a hut down the bank later on next morning. So that was the first good bit of news. And then we picked up, to our surprise, a radio message that 17 Platoon under Dennis Fox had captured the river bridge almost without firing a shot - the enemy had run away because of all the commotion - and 23 Platoon under 'Tod' Sweeney had reached them. Se there were two platoons over there and that was indeed very good news.

'As soon as I knew there were no explosives under the other bridge as well then we started sending out what has turned out to be a famous success signal, 'Ham and Jam'. 'Ham' for the canal bridge and 'Jam' for the river bridge captured intact. There were other code words, which meant they weren't captured or they were captured but blown up, but 'Ham' and 'Jam' were the important words as far as we were concerned. And that's the situation some fifteen or so minutes after landing.

'We knew the Germans were billeted in villages and always had somebody standing ready to counter-attack the bridges. They were known to have small tanks and lorries and be ready to get to the bridges, I was told, within an hour of our landing. The first movement was a motorcycle and what turned out to be a German staff car, rushing down the road from Ranville towards the river bridge. It crossed the bridge and then was shot up as planned and in that car was the German commander of the bridges, a Major Schmidt. The car came to a halt just between the bridges and the German commander, in perfect English, was shouting that he wanted to be shot. He said that he'd lost his honour, no doubt: meaning that his bridges had been captured. The doctor happened to be nearby, Doc John Vaughan and he gave him a couple of shots of morphine and put him to sleep.

'But it was while this was going on we heard the ominous sound - we most dreaded and that was the sound of tanks and, sure enough, round about half-past one, two tanks were heard slowly coming down the road. The only anti-tank weapons we had were PIATs and we didn't have much faith in them. Even under ideal conditions they had a maximum range of fifty yards. They threw a three-and-a-half pound bomb and, if it didn't hit directly whatever it was firing at, it had a nasty habit of not exploding and there wouldn't have been much time to reload, of course, with a tank under fifty yards away. We didn't like using them at night anyway. But the tanks came rumbling along.'

Major John Howard in command of 'D' Company, Ox and Bucks Light Infantry, Coup-de-main group for Pegasus Bridge.

'All the searchlights and flak was going up. They were firing into the night sky and it looked like a big firework display all along the French coast. As we approached the French coast, our six gliders were cast off. We were at about 5,000 feet and we went into the most horrendous dive I have ever done in a Horsa. We dived straight down - we had to get down quickly to get out of the range of the anti-aircraft guns. The idea was to trick the Germans into thinking they had gunned us down. We landed within about 75 yards of the canal bridge that we were after. The glider 'stove in', throwing the two pilots out of the cockpit. The rest of us were all knocked out for a second or two. There were about 30 German troops guarding the bridge over the canal and they were taken completely by surprise. I think only two or three Germans were up and about at that time on the other side of the bridge. One of them fired a Very light up into the night sky when we charged across the bridge, because he didn't know what the heck was happening and suddenly found himself facing all these guys with blackened faces charging across at him. Another one fired the machine gun that they had mounted there which unfortunately hit Denny Brotheridge, our platoon commander. He got a bullet through his neck and he died soon afterwards, which was very sad.

'We were throwing grenades around, I threw one or two and we were firing rifles literally up into the sky just to make a noise. The grenades I threw I aimed at the far side of the Caen Canal bank and they fell into the canal. Probably the only thing they killed were a few fish but they went off with quite a good bang. And the Germans literally ran. They scattered.'
Private Denis Edwards.

'I think we were all raring to go. I'd had the same platoon for over two years and only about three men in it had changed and we'd already had a great disappointment at the time of the Sicily invasion when we all went on embarkation leave but weren't actually chosen to go. We were keyed up, we were ready, we really didn't think we could do any more training and we wanted to get on with it and get into action for the first time. Although we knew D-Day was coming we thought that if we didn't get into action soon we'd never fire a bullet in anger. We were all briefed and kitted up and ready to go and then the whole operation was postponed. This was a severe shock to our morale, temporarily. And I, who don't normally drink much and another couple of officers bought two bottles of whisky which we demolished that night in our small tent.

'...Just after midnight on the morning of D-Day we were seated, arms interlocked, facing each other in silence, lest the enemy below were alerted by our voices. Not a sound, except for the swishing of air rushing past the open door of the Horsa glider, flying through the night at 90 mph over Normandy. Quite suddenly and unexpectedly the pilots said, 'Christ, there's the bridge' and they put the nose of the glider down very steeply. The next thing I knew was that there were sparks coming from the skids underneath. They didn't have wheels and I thought these sparks were actually enemy fire but they were in fact the skids striking the ground. A series of violent bumps and the sound of splintering wood, followed by my being ejected through the side of the glider but I wasn't in any way hurt. Relieved to find

I was still in one piece, still holding the Sten with its bayonet fixed and gratified that none of the extra grenades, which I was carrying in my camp kit canvas bucket had gone off. Pulled myself together, collected my platoon and doubled off to report to my Company Commander.

'The rest of the platoon got out of the glider. Some were like me thrown out and some got out through the doors. I collected them together. we knew exactly what we were supposed to do, although we didn't know at that moment whether we were the first glider to land or the second or the third, because three were destined to land at our particular bridge. I took the platoon forward to where I knew the bridge was and the road running up to it and there, crouching in the ditch, was my company commander, who said, quite simply, 'David, No 2.' And I knew that No 2's job was to cross the road and sort out the enemy on the other side in the inner defences of the bridge.

'The whole thing was over very quickly. I heard the magic words 'Ham and Jam' on my 38 set radio carried by my batman; and, as we were consolidating, my company commander came up on the radio and said I was to report to him on the road for further orders. So, taking my batman with me and the platoon sergeant, Sergeant Leather, I started to make my way back when I was hit in the leg by what turned out to be a burst of three rounds of Schmeisser machine pistol and fell to the ground quite unable to do anything. I was extremely frightened. I thought that at any minute the chap who'd fired at me was going to come along and finish me off, so I shouted, loudly. I didn't know at the time that both my batman and my platoon sergeant had been shot at the same time. But quite quickly a couple of men in the platoon came up and they did what they could for my leg, put a rifle splint on it and gave me some morphine and by then I was effectively out of the action.'

21-year old Lieutenant David J. Wood, 24th Platoon Commander, 'D' Company, 2nd Battalion, Oxfordshire and Buckinghamshire Light Infantry, Coup-de-main group for Pegasus Bridge. He was carried in a stretcher and taken to wait in a lane when there was a bang and a round went into the ground by his head. But rather than a shot from the sniper, it was a corporal who had drawn his gun to protect Colonel Wood and then accidentally set it off in his direction. After spending the night of D-Day sheltering in a barn under bombardment, Colonel Wood eventually arrived back in Southampton on 9 June.

Lieutenant Richard 'Sandy' Smith 14 Platoon, 'B' Company, 2nd Battalion, Oxfordshire and Buckinghamshire Light Infantry:
'I suppose there was a touch of apprehension but it was completely overruled by the wish to get on with it. We knew we were doing a very important job. We were told it was going to be an attack on two bridges and three gliders would have a go at one and three at the other. We were going to go in the night before and hold them for as long as possible until major reinforcements arrived and that would form the left flank of the invasion and we would keep away what armour and other German forces there were

on that side. As these two were the only bridges between the coast and Caen, which is a distance of eleven miles, it was pretty obvious that if we held those two bridges we could prevent the Germans from attacking the left flank of the major invasion. Hence its importance.

'One of the advantages we had was the fact that the operation would be a surprise, that we had the best glider pilots available and that they could land us exactly where they wanted to. And of course our ignorance of the hazards of the whole operation: we had no idea how risky it was because we had no experience of that sort of thing, so you can really say ignorance is bliss. I think some of the more experienced planners didn't really regard our operation as likely to be free of casualties. Indeed, I think we were called 'The Forlorn Hope' at one time. But it seemed to us a perfectly feasible thing to land on an enemy coast before D-Day, hold the two bridges. And the fact that there were eighty Germans on our bridge and a smaller number on the other, just five hundred yards apart, didn't seem to deter us, although our own strength of three gliders on the main bridge was somewhat less than the Germans holding it.

'We carried the normal airborne equipment, which meant you had an anti-tank PIAT as your sole defence against tanks. We carried two-inch mortars and Bren guns and the odd grenade, phosphorus and 36, Sten guns and the ordinary Enfield rifle. So it was pretty obvious to even the unimaginative that if we didn't get relief fairly quickly from the Paras, who were going to drop in the vicinity and subsequently from the commandos, who were coming from the coast six miles away, we were going to be in real trouble. The 21st Panzers were only a matter of half an hour away, stationed just the other side of Caen. Also the coastal forces had their own weaponry, plus tanks.

'My glider crashed rather badly in what you might call static water and smashed its whole front up. I was flung through the cockpit of the glider and ejected on to the ground, only to be over-run by the glider when it slithered to a halt and I had my knee rather badly damaged as a result of that because the wing or the undercarriage ran over me. I had a Lance Corporal Madge and I remember groping in the dark covered with mud and water and shock and he said, 'What are we waiting for, sir?' I tried to find my weapon and couldn't and found somebody else's Sten gun and ran towards the bridge. Or rather hobbled. Of my platoon, only about seven or eight were able to get out of that crash. Although they were not badly hurt they were very, very shocked and bruised. One man was killed.

'I found a Spandau firing right down the centre of the bridge, so I swept left, down the catwalk running along the side of the bridge, to avoid this machine gun and arrived at the other end to find Brotheridge dying. And then in the flurry I remember a German throwing a stick grenade at me and I saw the explosion, felt the explosion. My right wrist was hit. I was extremely lucky because the grenade exploded very close to me and hit various parts of my clothing but not my body, although there were holes in my smock. And that was the first German I actually shot. Having thrown his grenade, he tried to scramble over the back of one of the walls adjoining the cafe and I actually shot him with my Sten gun as he went over.

'I took over Brotheridge's platoon and put them in a defensive position round the far end of the bridge, the one nearest the village of Le Port and gathered what was left of my platoon and put them in together with Brotheridge's platoon. Then I went back to the other side of the bridge, only to be told that David Wood's platoon were leaderless because he'd been shot through the legs. I reported back to John Howard and said Wood was wounded and Brotheridge was dead or dying and I'd been knocked about a bit and he told me to go back and organise the defence at the far end of the bridge, which I did. After a while the Germans had recovered from the initial shock and surprise and they were coming down from the village of Le Port, a matter of two or three hundred yards and started to infiltrate through the backs of houses and gardens towards the bridge and they started making it obvious that they were going to do something.

'So there I was, as the only officer on his feet, with these three platoons. I felt rather exposed so I went back to Howard, who was stationed between the two bridges and I said to him, 'Look, I wouldn't mind another platoon. If there's no trouble on the other bridge, could you please send me one of those two platoons?' Denis Fox arrived, much to my relief, marching up through the bridge and I told him to go up to the village of Le Port, where there's a small crossroads and to hold that so at least we'd have some idea of what the Germans were trying to do. I remember him saying to me, 'I haven't got an anti-tank PIAT,' because he'd left it in his glider in a hurry and I said, 'Well, take mine,' which we had extricated from our crashed glider. And I remember him saying, 'Well, thanks for nothing.' He took this PIAT and handed it over to Sergeant Thornton and took up a position near the crossroads at Le Port.

'I heard, to my horror, the rattle of tank tracks coming down the road from the Le Port direction. And I remember feeling very, very hopeless because there we were without an anti-tank weapon, except for the one we'd given to Dermis, with my platoon only about seven or eight strong and Brotheridge's twenty-odd people. I thought, 'Well, this is going to be it' and I vividly remember the troops looking at me to see whether I was reacting in any way to the arrival of this tank. And I remember my order: 'Look to your front.' What else I could have said I don't know. I gave that order because they wanted some form of reassurance, though I must confess that I didn't really feel very reassured myself. Anyway, a minute or two later the rumbling of this tank was heard to be getting louder and louder and then there was a sharp explosion as Sergeant Thornton, as I subsequently discovered, had fired at it at point-blank range.'

'The PIAT actually was a load of rubbish, really. The range is around about fifty yards and no more. You're a dead loss if you try to go farther. Even fifty yards is stretching it, very much so. Another thing is that you must never, never miss. If you do, you've had it, because by the time you reload the thing and cock it, which is a bloody chore on its own, everything's gone, you're done. It's indoctrinated into your brain that you mustn't miss.'
Sergeant 'Wagger' Thornton.

'Wagger' let these tanks get really up close to him and then he let fly' continues **Private Denis Edwards, 25 Platoon, 'D' Company.** 'We never thought those PIAT bombs would ever do much damage to a proper tank but this flaming tank literally blew up, exploded. The whole thing went up. It was well loaded with ammunition. I don't know what sort of ammunition, but within moments of 'Wagger' firing there were great spurts of green and orange and yellow as all the ammunition inside was exploding, making a hell of a din. And the other tank behind did a quick revving of engines and disappeared, backed off up the road and we never heard from them again.'

'It blew up, fortunately, right on the crossroads, blocking the entrance to the bridge either way, killing most of the crew and one poor soul was flung out and his legs had almost disappeared and he subsequently died. I had to pass him every time I went up to see how Dennis Fox was getting on and I remember Dennis saying to me 'Look, why don't you shoot that fellow, because he's disturbing my men.' And I just couldn't shoot him.

'The Germans then started infiltrating down the backs of the gardens away from the crossroads to try and come into us from either side, from the canal, down through the towpaths on either side. So we withdrew ourselves to a much closer defensive position around the head of the bridge and I tried to give the impression that we were much stronger than we were by moving Bren gun sections from one position to another and firing off tracer into the dark. It seemed to have some effect. It kept the Germans away from us and we didn't really have any what you might call hand-to-hand scrapping. It was really more them trying to find out what the hell was going on.

'I remember lying in a ditch in this little gully-way between the two bridges having my wrist bandaged by one of our first aid people and a sniper bullet came cracking over my right shoulder. It hit this fellow in the chest - he was actually bending over me - and knocked him clear into the road. The bullet went straight through him. I remember him lying in the middle of the road and I expected the next bullet from the sniper to come and get me on the back of the neck because I couldn't get any lower. That wasn't a very pleasant moment.'

'The poor buggers in the bunkers didn't have much of a chance and we were not taking any prisoners or messing around, we just threw phosphorous grenades down and high explosive grenades into the dugouts there and anything that moved we shot.'
Lieutenant Richard 'Sandy' Smith.

'Claude and I were twin brothers and members of No.2 Platoon, 249 Field Company, Royal Engineers, attached to 'D' Company, Ox and Bucks Light Infantry. We were under the command Major John Howard, Ox and Bucks and Captain Jock Neilson, Royal Engineers. Gliders 1, 2 and 3 would land on the Canal Bridge and gliders 4, 5 and 6 on the Orne bridge. Claude and I were both in No.6 glider - I'll bet there weren't many twins in that position that night! With blackened faces and hands we got aboard. The doors closed and then we heard the increased power of the engines of the Halifax and then the jerk of the tow rope and we were off! The gliders left at one-minute intervals into the night sky. Thirty men in each glider, five of whom were Royal Engineers. For most of us this was our first time in action and there was almost no conversation in the blacked out interior of the glider. No lights at all were permitted. We flew at 6,000 feet with fighter aircraft escort and crossed the French coast a few minutes after midnight. Suddenly we felt our glider being released and then seemingly in minutes we had landed with grunts and groans from both our bucking plywood aircraft and ourselves!

'I had been detailed to check that after we landed everyone had left the glider and so I jumped out from the rear-side door, ran a few yards and flattened myself on French soil. And nobody else was there! Just a few staring cows four or five yards from me and otherwise complete silence! Where had all my mates gone and where were the other two gliders? For a second I thought I might be a one-man invasion force and so I moved ahead of the glider and found to my relief a bunch of men kneeling by a hedge. 'Scout Section,' I whispered. 'Shut up' was the reply. So I moved ahead and there found the others from my glider and we all moved off at a fair pace, down into a ditch, up the other side and on to a road and there straight ahead of us was 'our bridge'.

'One shot was all we heard from the enemy and one of our men threw a smoke bomb. In the same instant we charged across the bridge. As we did that the sappers were checking for electric wires that would lead to explosive charges as Intelligence Reports had stated that the bridges had been prepared for demolition. Guns were now firing on the Canal bridge 400 yards away but all I heard from the 'defenders' of our bridge was the sound of running feet down the tow-path! The sound of 30 pairs of British Army hob-nailed boots rushing around in the darkness was enough to scare the bravest hearts! But how far would they have gone and where to?

'I went under the bridge to the water's edge and in the patchy cloudy moonlight saw a huge dark object right under the centre of the bridge. A barge filled with explosives? A continuation of single width scaffold boards had been laid through the girders into the darkness. 'That's where the explosive will be,' I thought. 'Phew.' So I called for support and lo and behold my twin brother appeared alongside me. Apparently whilst I was under the bridge all other personnel had moved off. So we went to investigate. Crawling through the girders with rifle and back pack was no joke and the water rushing below me was not inviting either. The 'dark object' turned out to be a huge brick pier containing the bridge opening equipment and, thankfully, no explosives. They were discovered next day in a nearby shed.

'Whilst under the bridge we heard running feet above us. Hopefully from the other gliders, but we weren't going to check! I put out my torch and waited and when it was silent Claude and I climbed back on to the road. It was 30 minutes since we had landed and as we got on to the road we saw the first paras dropping and then amazingly, from somewhere in the distance the 'All Clear' sounded. They didn't know we were there! Claude and I made our way cautiously to the Canal Bridge, which had by now been captured and waited for the inevitable German counter attack. But all we saw before dawn was a German Foot patrol, staff car and motorcycle which were quickly finished off by the infantry on the river bridge. A sole German tank approached the Canal Bridge but that was quickly destroyed with a PIAT bomb.

'Early dawn saw a number of Lancaster bombers twisting and turning very low over a coastal gun battery prior to an attack by the 6th Airborne and a naval bombardment could clearly be heard. Daylight now and we saw and learned of our casualties. One officer killed, one soldier drowned, six wounded and one glider (No.4) missing. Our glider had been the first to land at the river bridge - hence my being on my own initially!

'Then we saw two German naval craft cautiously approaching upstream to the Canal Bridge and we opened fire. From my slit-trench I only managed to fire one round at the wheelhouse before my gun jammed. I had managed to get grit into and over my rifle bolt! But it caused no problems. The boat grounded and the crew surrendered and Claude went aboard to check everything out. The second craft managed to turn back but I presume would have been finished off shortly afterwards by the beach landing troops.

'A little later in the morning now and we were getting problems! There were German snipers in the trees and the Church Tower and buildings were in use by German troops. The fire was becoming heavy and accurate. We had limited heavy equipment, but the Ox and Bucks had got hold of a German anti-tank gun together with ammunition and started to use it with some success against the Church tower. Whilst we were now getting some heavy fire on the bridge I saw Allied fighter aircraft flying overhead quite unmolested! Very frustrating!'

Sapper Cyril Larkin. He and his twin brother Claude were born in Auckland, New Zealand in 1917. Their parents returned to England in 1920-21 and after leaving school both twins were keen to return to New Zealand but the war put paid to this. In 1939 they tried to join the New Zealand Army via New Zealand House in London but the following February they were called up for the British Army.

'We were a bunch of young men, weighed down with guns and equipment, our faces blackened. We literally dropped out of the night sky behind enemy lines. I knew thousands of men were landing on the Normandy beaches. We might have been a total disaster but as a psyched up 23-year-old you don't think of such things. Because I was one of the first to make the drop I suppose I'm thought of as hero. I'm not. To me the real heroes were the many thousands of soldiers I saw fight so very gallantly. Some did not come back. Shortly after I landed my best friend, Captain Bobby Delatour (also an actor) was killed only five or six yards away from me. When we managed to cross the first bridge and were on our way to the second bridge, one of the gliders went straight into a German tank, which blew up, sky-high.

The first few aircraft got in with a certain amount of surprise factor on their side but after that, many of them were shot down. I was damned lucky.

7 Para suffered very heavy casualties. Some were captured. Some were killed in the air before they got to the ground. Others were killed fighting their way through. We dropped 610 men. By the morning of D-Day there were 240 left. 'A' Company had borne the brunt of the attack. In 'C' Company, who were more or less next to 'A' Company, all the officers were killed and there were only 20 men remaining. 'B' Company did better as far as officers were concerned, but had more lost on the ground. When we were relieved we dug in for the night in the area of Ranville to the east of the River Orne and Caen Canal. That night we were quite heavily attacked with guns coming from Bréville. On D+1 we had quite a little firefight, then on the second half of the day we were ordered to move to Le Mesnil, to clear quite a large area of orchard and field.

I think possibly the most unsung person of the day was Colonel Pine-Coffin. He was not only the man who trained 7 Para Battalion, but he also controlled them and remained cool, calm and collected.

23 year old First Lieutenant Richard Todd, 7th Light Infantry Battalion, 5th Parachute Brigade, the star of many post war film epics such as *The Dam Busters, Yangtse Incident* and *The Longest Day* (when he played the part of Colonel Howard). (From a total of five officers and 120 men originally in 'A' Company, there were no surviving officers and fewer than 20 men by the middle of 6 June). Then, under the command of Colonel Geoffrey Pine-Coffin, held a pocket until late in the evening of D-Day, until a battalion of the Warwickshire regiment who had been seaborne, relieved them in turn.

'All one could see were other parachutists blundering about as lost as oneself. The Germans were there, too, firing tracer ammunition. Officers and others collected parties and began to search systematically but it was a question of the blind leading the blind. It was an hour and a half before I found the rendezvous for my party and we were the first there even then. My rallying signal was a bugle and luckily my bugler was with me and Private Lambert sounded off continuously and we waited and hoped. They came in as fast as they could but it seemed desperately slow and there was practically none of the heavy gear with them. No sound came from the bridges. I decided to move off when I reached half-strength but this took so long that I gave the order earlier. No mortars, machine guns or wireless had arrived so we would just have to do without them. The coup de main party's success signal went up just as we moved off and put new life into us. Half the job had been done: the bridges had been captured.'

Lieutenant Colonel Geoffrey Pine-Coffin, Commanding Officer, 7th Battalion, Parachute Regiment.

'On the evening of June 5th, as the last glow of twilight was fading from the western sky, six RAF Albemarles were drawn up on the runway of Harwell airfield. Gathered around them, drinking tea and smoking cigarettes, were 60 men of the 22nd Independent Parachute Company, pathfinders who were to guide the 6th Airborne Division to its landfall behind the Atlantic Wall near Caen. Their faces and equipment were smeared with brown, black and green paint and over their uniforms they wore camouflaged jumping smocks. Every man was a walking arsenal. They had crammed so much ammunition into their pockets and pouches, so many weapons into their webbing that they had found it difficult to hitch on their parachute harnesses. Grenades were festooned about them; they had fighting knives in their gaiters and clips of cartridges in the linings of their steel helmets. No man was carrying less than 85 lbs: some more than a hundred and in addition each had strapped to his leg a 60lb kitbag containing lights and radar beacons with which to mark the dropping and landing zones for the rest of the division.

'These men were the torchbearers of liberation. Like all paratroops they were volunteers and they had been specially picked and trained; for this responsible task, but otherwise there was little to distinguish them from the rest of Montgomery's force. Beside the leading aircraft were the ten men who were due to land first, at the point of the invasion spearhead, a Berkshire hod-carrier and a toolmaker from Kent, a bricklayer from Edinburgh, a Worcestershire kennelman and a lorry driver from Dumfries, two 'regulars,' a deserter from the 'army' of the Irish Free State and a refugee from Austria, led by a young lieutenant, who, when war began, had been in the chorus of a West End musical comedy. Three of them had been at Dunkirk, one had fought in Africa, but the rest were going into battle for the first time.

'These pathfinders were the vanguard of the force that had the most vital role in the 'Neptune' plan - that of seizing and holding the left flank of the bridgehead-the open flank, against which the main weight of German counter-attack was likely to fall as the panzer divisions moved in from their garrison areas south-east and east of Caen. If 6th Airborne were to fail, the whole bridgehead might be rolled up from this wing before the seaborne divisions could become firmly established.

'...Riding behind an Albemarle tug we are scudding through clouds which shroud moon and ground alike. There is soft rain on the perspex of the cockpit and all we can see is the guiding light in the tail of the tug, until a break in the clouds gives us a brief glimpse of the south coast from which the invasion fleet has long since sailed. Half-way across the Channel it clears again and we can see the dark, stormy water, flecked with the wake of countless ships. More cloud and we are flying blind again at 2,500 feet. The glider begins to pitch and bucket in the gusty wind that threatens to sunder the tow-rope and leave us drifting helpless in the sky. But this is a minor worry compared with those that lie ahead.

'Does the enemy know we are coming? What will the flak be like? Are there mines and booby-traps as well as obstructions on the landing-zone? Will the paratroops have had time to clear it? Will a battle be raging there already as we come in to land? Will the pilots ever find it in this weather?

'If these thoughts are also running through the minds of the other 26 officers and men sitting in the dark fuselage of the glider, they show I no sign of it. Above the steady roar of the wind beating on the glider's wooden surface, you can hear a snatch of song or a gust of laughter.

'Three o'clock: half an hour to go. The clouds clear for a minute and we are warned of the closeness of the coast-and of another tug and glider which has cut across our bow, perilously near. Away to our left the RAF is bombing enemy batteries near Le Havre and the sky is lit by the burst of bombs and flash of guns until the clouds shut us in again. Now when we need a clear sky, it is thicker than ever and at times we lose sight even of the tug's tail light. Suddenly the darkness is stabbed with streaks of light, red and yellow tracer from the flak guns on the coast. There are four sharp flashes between us and the tug and then another that seems to be inside the glider itself. It is, but we don't realise at first that we have been hit, for the shell has burst harmlessly well aft beyond the farthest seats. The tug begins to weave but it can't take violent evasive action lest the towrope should snap.

'Over the coast we run out of the cloud and there below us is the white curving strand of France and, mirrored in the dim moonlight, the twin ribbons of water we are looking for - the Orne and the Canal. The tug has taken us right to the target, but we can't pick out the lights, which are to mark the landing-zone. There is so much flak firing from the ground that it's hard to tell what the flashes are and before the pilots can identify any landmarks we are into the cloud again.

'Soon one of them turns and calls back to us - 'I'm letting go, hold tight.' As it leaves the tug the glider seems to stall and to hover like a hawk about to strike. The roar of the wind on the wooden skin drops to a murmur with the loss of speed and there is a strange and sudden silence. We are floating in a sky of fathomless uncertainty - in suspense between peace and war. We are through the flak-belt and gliding so smoothly that the fire and turmoil of battle seem to belong to another world.

'We are jerked back to reality by a sharp, banking turn and we are diving steeply, plunging down into the darkness. As the ground rises up to meet us, the pilots catch a glimpse of the pathfinders' lights and the white dusty road and the square Norman church-tower beside the landing-zone. The stick comes back and we pull out of the dive with sinking stomachs and bursting ears. The glider is skimming the ground now with plenty of speed on and is about to land when out of the night another glider comes straight for us. We 'take-off' again, lift sharply and it sweeps under our nose. The soil of France rushes past beneath us and we touch-down with a jolt on a ploughed field. It is rough and soft, but the glider careers on with grinding brakes and creaking timbers, mowing down 'Rommel's asparagus' and snapping off five stout posts in its path. There is an ominous sound of splitting wood and rending fabric and we brace ourselves for the shock as the glider goes lurching and bumping until with a violent swerve to starboard it finally comes to rest scarred but intact, within a hundred yards of its intended landing place.

'It is 0332. We are two minutes late. Shouts and cheers echo down the glider and a voice from the dark interior cries out, 'This is it, chum. I told yer we wouldn't 'av ter swim.'

'We scramble out into a cornfield, which is the graveyard of many

gliders. Some have buried their noses in the soft soil, others have lost a
wing, a wheel or a complete undercarriage, several have broken their backs,
one has crashed into a house and two have crashed into each other. Few
have come through with as little damage as ours and all around us the
twisted wrecks make grotesque silhouettes against the sky, now lit by a
burst of flame as the petrol' tanks of a crashing aircraft explode.

'The wreckage seems to signify the failure of the daring plan to land the
gliders by night, but in fact, though we don't yet know it, 49 of the 72
destined for this field have landed accurately and, despite the chaos and
the damage, the casualties to men and weapons are comparatively few.
Indeed as we move off towards the rendezvous near Ranville church, men
are climbing out of the broken wrecks, dragging their equipment and
slashing away the splintered fuselages to set free jeeps and guns. Ten of the
eighteen anti-tank guns have survived and soon they are moving to their
appointed positions.

'The flak guns are still firing spasmodically into an empty sky, but
otherwise there is little sight or sound of fighting. It seems unreal to be
talking about behind the Atlantic Wall unhindered by the enemy and every
moment we expect to hear a shot or challenge ring out of the darkness. In
the absence of noise of nearby battle every sound is magnified. The rustle
of troops moving through high corn, the muttered curse from a stumbling
man, the crash of an axe on flimsy wood, the roar of a jeep engine, the
rumble of a gun-carriage, carry far in the night, at the expected crack and
thunder of guns is missing. The only challenge is from our own paratroops
dug in on the edge of the landing-zone. To their call of 'V for,' we quickly
add the other half of the password - 'Victory.'

'That is all, until we reach the road near Ranville church, from which
there comes an outburst of fire and counter-fire, followed by the sound of
German voices, the roar of a departing car, a burst from a Tommy-gun and
then silence. The column of men on the road moves smartly to the cover of
a hedgerow, expecting any minute to make contact with a German patrol.
We lie there quiet and alert, picturing the enemy moving stealthily towards
us from the direction of the church. But the sound that splits the silence is
an unmistakable voice, booming out: 'Don't you dare to argue with me -
Richard Gale. Get on, I say, get on.'

'In the faint half-light we can now make out a halted column of jeeps
and guns close by on a side-road with Gale himself urging them on. And,
walking a little fractiously beside the column, shepherded by the General's
aide-de-camp, is a handsome chestnut horse which had been grazing on the
landing-zone.

'Take care of that animal, Tommy!' says Gale, 'It's a fine morning for a ride.'

'Gale set up his HQ in a château at Ranville. In the grounds the chestnut
horse and a dozen sleek cows cropped the rich grass, somewhat disturbed
by explosions on all sides as the airborne troops blew slit-trenches for
themselves with plastic charges. These made such a noise that the occasional
whine of a sniper's bullet or the crump of a mortar-bomb passed almost
unheeded. But the predominant note in this medley was the gobbling of a

flock of turkeys which had taken refuge in a large tree and felt constrained to give throat in answer to each explosion.

'Into this bedlam rode Gale in a jeep, fresh from a visit to the captured bridges. At the top of the front steps he paused and looked around his newly-won domain, across the fields strewn with parachutes of many colours and, across the glider landing-zone to the wooded ridge where already, he hoped, the 3rd Parachute Brigade was established. As he turned in through the door, he muttered, half to himself,

And gentlemen in England now a-bed
Shall think themselves accurs'd they were not here.'

The Struggle For Europe by Chester Wilmot, famed Australian correspondent. Having previously covered Australian operations in North Africa and on the Kokoda Track, he had transferred to Europe. Working for the BBC, he accompanied the 6th Airborne Division into Normandy, landing in a glider flown by Lieutenant Colonel Ian Murray carrying Brigadier the Hon. Hugh Kindersley, Commanding the 6th Air Landing Brigade and some of his staff. Soon after landing it was found that Wilmot's recorder had been smashed by a piece of shell from an ack-ack gun. Certainly one of the first Australians to land in France on D-Day, his reporting from the battlefield thrilled his radio audience in Britain and further afield. His recording of the chiming of the church bells of the first village liberated in France was heard around the world. Chester Wilmot died in the crash of a Comet airliner in 1954.

'A Dulwich schoolmaster, turned glider-pilot, landed General Richard Gale in a ploughed field. Dust and earth forced its way up into the big black Horsa. A landing wheel was whipped off in a ditch; the glider hit a post and swivelled round on its nose. 'Fine work, my boy,' said the general and stepped out. All tried to free the general's jeep from the twisted wreckage but could not do so. They got out of the field and crossed waist-high through a crop of corn to the village road. Through the village was the country house that the general had picked from a map as his temporary headquarters. When they got there, Griffith kicked open the door and lurched in with his Tommy gun, his eyes peeled for Germans. Inside were two pairs of short-sighted eyes, peering out from the faces of two spinster ladies in their nightdresses, who held candles up at him and said, 'Bon jour'. Soon they were fussing over the general who began fixing his communications. Then the two old ladies insisted on serving him a breakfast of bacon and eggs.

'All the primary paratroop objectives had been taken. The general ordered his Red Devils to dig in and 'infest the area'. Gale's batman, concerned that 'his general' should have suitable transportation, spotted a chestnut mare not far from the Horsa. Off he went and soon had his general mounted in true cavalry style. The general badly needed some means of transport over the tricky farmland with its hedges and woods. The horse was 'just the job'.

'At the dawn muster the troops found the general walking the horse round the garden of his headquarters. He tied her up among the jeeps that had collected in the courtyard. but on her next journey out, she got hit by shrapnel.'

James E. Mrazek [7]

'On D-Day the BBC had reporters with the forces moving in on each of the landing beaches. Chester Wilmot landed with the Glider force. Guy Byams dropped with the Paras. BBC correspondents flew with the Allied fighter and bomber formations. Others were at sea with the naval forces and the merchant ships. It was a thoroughly comprehensive coverage. In all, the BBC reporting staff for the Normandy campaign numbered 27, with the support of 33 engineer colleagues. But with it all and historic as the operation was in broadcasting terms, we were, of course, only the messengers. We were unarmed observers, living and moving with the men who won the victory. But we, too, took our casualties. We were proud when Field Marshal Montgomery wrote to the BBC at the end of hostilities, saying '...these correspondents made no mean contribution to final victory'.'

Frank Gillard CBE, senior BBC war correspondent.[8] The BBC, stung by criticism of its inadequate coverage of earlier campaigns in the Middle East, fielded no less than 19 top commentators, including famous names like Gillard, Wilmot, Richard Dimbleby, Michael Standing, Guy Byams and Canadians Stanley Maxted and Stewart MacPherson. They were given combat training and brought to a peak of physical fitness. To enable the reporters to get close to the action, a lightweight disc recorder had been designed by BBC engineers, weighing only 40 pounds.

In the early years of the war Guy Byams saw action with the RNVR and Combined operations but was wounded and invalided out. He joined the BBC War Reporting Unit in April 1944. He landed with the British Paratroops on D-Day morning:
'In the crowded fuselage all you see in the pale light of an orange bulb is the man next to you.

'And you fly out over the Channel and the minutes go by and the stock

---

7 *The Glider War* by James E. Mrazek (Robert Hale & Co 1975).
8   From 19 June onward, Creully, a small township about six kilometres from the beaches was the operational base for all the broadcast reporting of the ground fighting. Until 19 August, when the Battle of Normandy was officially and finally won, the tower room of the Château of Creully was undoubtedly the busiest studio of the entire BBC anywhere. In addition to the BBC's correspondents, the radio reporters of all the Allied nations used the studio. A small team of censors was permanently attached to us, to prevent delays and holdups. Reports, despatches, actuality recordings from the thick of the battles, poured out from this small centre in a constant stream, day and night, and in many tongues. The BBC alone was broadcasting to the world, directly and by language translation in 49 languages. Add to that the vast audiences reached by all the allied broadcasters, whose messages form their own correspondents were reaching them from Creully via the BBC in London. In total, probably the greatest aggregate audiences ever consistently achieved by radio internationally came from the small tower at Creully, bringing the glorious news of mounting Allied triumph to all our friends and shattering the last hopes of our foes, to whom the words they heard must indeed have seemed 'more deadly than steel'.'

commander says that the pilot has told him we are over a great armada of naval ships. And then it is something else he says - something that gives you a dry feeling in your mouth - flak - and the word is passed from man to man. The machine starts to rock and jump with it. Ahead of us - a comforting thought - Lancasters are going for the flak and a coastal battery is one of the objectives.

'The run has started - one minute and thirty seconds. Red light - green and out - get on, out, out fast into the cool night air, out, out, out over France - and we know that the dropping zone is obstructed. We're jumping into fields covered with poles! And I hit my parachute and lower my kitbag which is suspended on the end of a forty foot rope from my harness. And then the ground comes up to hit me. And I find myself in the middle of a cornfield. I look around and even with a compass I can't be sure where I am - and overhead hundreds of parachutes and containers are coming down. The whole sky is a fantastic chimera of lights and flak and one plane gets hit and disintegrates wholesale in the sky, sprinkling a myriad of burning pieces all over the sky.

'On the dropping zone, shock paratroop engineers are finishing blowing the poles that obstruct the dropping zone and soon the gliders come in scores, coming out of the sky like a sign.

'And the night wears on and soon it is light and to the northwest the cannonade begins on the beaches. While our paratroop unit fights a terrific battle over the bridges) actually repelling an attack by a Panzer formation - paratroops able to deal with the Panzers. I think that one surprised the German High Command. These airborne units fight magnificently with terrific morale and vigour.

'The people are pleased to see us. We apologize for the bringing of war to their homes. But in little ways they show they are glad to see us. A dead paratroop is laid out on a bed in the best bedroom covered from head to foot with local flowers.'

Reports like this made Guy Byams a household name. On 3 February 1945 Byams was killed on B-17G *The Rose of York* in the 306th Bomb Group, 8th Air Force over Berlin on a daylight raid with the 8th Air Force. A listener wrote after his death: 'All looked forward to hearing his enthusiastic and youthful voice in the 9 o'clock news.'

'Their faces were darkened with cocoa; sheathed knives were strapped to their ankles: Tommy guns strapped to their waists; bandoliers and hand grenades, coils of rope, pick handles, spades, rubber dinghies hung around them and a few personal elements, like the lad who was taking a newspaper to read on the plane. I watched them march in a long, snaking, double line, almost a mile long, to draw their parachutes. Later, I saw them gathered around their C-47 aircraft and making final adjustments to their kit before they started. There was an easy familiar touch about the way they were getting ready as if they had done it often before. Well, yes, they had kitted up and climbed aboard often just like this - twenty, thirty, forty times some of them. But it had never been quite like this before. This was the first combat jump for every one of them.'

Robert Barr of the BBC with British Paratroops on the eve of D-Day, broadcast on 6 June 1944.

'Of enemy troop movements there was, until noon today, little or no sign from the air, even close to the immediate battle area. Long stretches of empty roads shining with rain, deserted dripping woods and damp fields - static, quiet - perhaps uncannily quiet - and possibly not to remain quiet. But here and there a movement catches the eye, as our aircraft on reconnaissance roar over a large suspicious wood - three German soldiers running like mad across the main road to fling themselves into cover. And near the battle area, much nearer the battle area than they, a solitary peasant harrowing his field, up and down behind the horses, looking nowhere but before him and the soil.

The British, Canadian and American troops who landed on the coast of France north of the lovely town of Caen in broad daylight this morning, are already several miles inland, on a front sufficiently broad to be more than a bridgehead. They're pushing steadily on backed by the tremendous fire-power of heavy British and United States warships and covered-by an ever-changing but ever present umbrella of fighters. The first phase of the great operation began about midnight last night, when a force of parachutists and glider troops, some of which I saw taking off in the dying light of yesterday, landed on the eastern side of the chosen area to secure that flank.

'Today, the gliders and some of the discarded parachutes lie like crumpled flowers in the wet, wooded countryside north-east of Caen. Evidence enough that our airborne troops have successfully completed this, the first of their operations in the new battle of Europe.

'The first parties ashore this morning worked at splendid speed. By half-past-ten, quite apart from the Sappers, the infantry and the tanks already pushing into France, there were two sizeable bulldozers ashore, working on a stretch of road that may well become the Royal Air Force's first landing strip in France and it's going to be ready very soon for the fighters to use.

'It's too early yet, much too early, to start giving any reasons for the comparative lack of resistance put up by the Germans to our initial landing, but most certainly the first foothold was attained more easily than anyone had dared to hope. This time we have 'cashed-in' on our success and wave after wave of landing craft have been crossing the Channel, unloading reinforcements and stores and armour. Our tanks can be seen moving inland not far from the immediate battle area... Here and there a movement catches the eye; a pathetic little procession of civilian refugees, cars loaded with furniture and bundles and all the domestic animals around them, making away from Caen...'

Richard Dimbleby, BBC Commentator who flew on the operation to France had telephoned his report back to London at 4.15 on 6 June. That evening, at 9.30pm it was broadcast to the British nation huddled around their wireless sets.

'We took off and sat in silence for a while, just listening to the roar of the wind and the tow aircraft's engines. We were soon over the French coast and all hell started up, the anti aircraft fire exploded in the night sky, we called the shells 'Flaming Onions' because of the way they looked and came towards us in a string. I looked around me and for once, no one was being airsick. I was scared stiff and yet excited in anticipation of what lay ahead of us.

'Suddenly, the towrope was released by the glider pilot and we were away on our own, just the rush of the wind and the downward spiral to France and our fate. In what seemed only a few minutes the words, 'Brace, Brace, Brace' were shouted and we all linked arms, awaiting the impact of the landing. Sparks seemed to stream down the fuselage and we touched down, screeching and crashing, till suddenly we came to a stop. We didn't bother to open the door of the Horsa; we just all seemed to pile out through the gashes in the fuselage. I grabbed a trolley full of mortar bombs and pulled for all my worth, only for one to fall out and smash my toe. Someone else came over to give me a hand and we ran towards the bridge. It is very hard to explain to anyone the feelings of war, exhilaration, fear, excitement and comradeship towards your fellow troops who you have been with for the past months.

I ran to the edge of the road leading to the bridge filled with a feeling of apprehension of what was going to happen. I must have had a guardian angel watching over me because I was still there with so much death around me. Bullets were flying everywhere. I heard the cry, 'Medic' and I ran towards a guy lying at the side of the road. As I ran, I looked to my left and saw a German soldier running the same way. We were both trying to survive, not knowing why we were doing what we were doing.

'In just a couple of minutes I had injured men who had been hurt in the crash landing. I herded three men into a hedgerow to treat their wounds. I was in that ditch for hours because we could not cross the bridge until the snipers had been found. It was about 8 am before I eventually transferred them to the café and relative safety. I saw a small French girl, ashen faced and scared to hell. I reached into my tunic and gave her my bar of chocolate, but still she did not smile. Then I joined up with about half a dozen other men who were making their way to Ranville to rejoin their own companies when the rest of regiment came in on the dropping zones. It had been hours since I saw a familiar face.

'The guys had taken several prisoners at the bridge. One was a young boy of 16. I crossed the Orne Bridge and passed a Para with six prisoners and later rejoined 'B' Company as we all regrouped at Ranville for the attack on Escoville. We set up our mortars in an orchard near a farmhouse with a long driveway. I dug a trench and felt uneasy so I moved to another spot and soon after we were heavily mortar bombed, suffering many casualties. Three men from our mortar squad were severely wounded. A bomb had landed in my original trench. What made me move I do not know.

'Later we moved to the woods at Château St Côme. We all stepped over a German soldier lying dead across the path leading into the wood. I will never forget the awful carnage caused when the battleship Warspite opened fire on these woods not knowing the Black Watch of the 51st Highland Division had already cleared it of Germans. The smell of death hung over the place. Dead bodies were everywhere. It was terrible and the stench made one feel sick. Everywhere, dead horses and cows were bloating up. There was an awful smell when someone put a bullet in one of them and they burst. It was a smell of death that none can describe but will never forget.

'I dug a trench only to find water seeping in. We were shelled, mortared and machine gunned during the day and sometimes bombed at night but the worst were the air burst mortar bombs, which showered shrapnel down on top of us and caused many casualties. There was turmoil when 'D' Company was cut off and 'B' Company put in an attack to get them out. We had orders to withdraw and as we pulled out up a gully a German threw a stick grenade over the hedge, which severely wounded Sergeant Stan Bridges in his upper arm. I bandaged and splinted his arm and eventually got him to safety when we were sent back about three fields behind the front line for a rest. It was a nightmare. One bomb landed a few yards from my trench and the concussion caused the side of my trench to collapse on me. I was half buried and really scared stiff. We moved back into the woods but it was chaos.

'During these actions I came across some horrible injuries. The worst was the one where a piece of shrapnel had hit this man in the corner of his mouth and tore a gash to his ear. The side of his face fell down to his neck and looked an awful mess. I gave him a shot of morphine and then put a roll of lint along his gums. Then I pinned his face up with four safety pins, applied a dressing held on with Elastoplasts and got him evacuated to the casualty clearing station.

'I was wounded in the head by an air burst shell as I ran to help Sergeant Bobby Hill who had also been wounded. There was a blinding flash and I fell on top of him. He bandaged me up and got me evacuated to Bayeux. A piece of shrapnel had pierced the top of my helmet and blown a big hole in the top of my head. How I survived all this hell, only God knows. I regained consciousness in a C-47 Dakota while crossing the Channel back to England. A young nurse said, 'The war's over for you my lad'! I lost consciousness again and the next thing I remember is waking up in a military hospital in Oxford, with my wife looking down on me. It was only then that I realised I would be all right.'

Albert Gregory RAMC **'B' Company, 2nd Oxfordshire and Buckinghamshire Regiment, who was with the remainder of the Battalion during the evening of D-Day.**

'People of Western Europe, A landing was made this morning on the coast of France by troops of the Allied Expeditionary Force. This landing is part of a concerted United Nations plan for the liberation of Europe, made in conjunction with our great Russian allies. I have this message for all of you, although the initial assault may not have been in your own country, the hour of your liberation is approaching.'

General Dwight D. Eisenhower Broadcast to Europe, June 6.

American Airborne troops preparing to board their C-47 transport.

Among the first of the airborne troops to land in France were four officers of the 22nd Independent Parachute Company. They are, left to right, Captain Bobby de La Tour and Lieutenant Don Wells, both from London and Lieutenants John Vischer, Newport Pagnell and Bob Midwood, Scarborough, seen setting their watches before taking off. Captain de La Tour was KIA on 20 June only five or six yards away from Richard Todd.

American airborne troops in their C-47.

B-26B 42-96142 *Dee-Feater* in the 596th Bomb Squadron, 397th Bomb Group at Rivenhall flown by Lieutenant Colonel Robert L. McLeod, the squadron CO. The aircraft was named in honour of McLeod's wife Dee and it acted as the lead ship on many missions in the summer of 1944. McLeod flew 27 missions as box leader from Rivenhall, many of them in *Dee-Feater.* (USAF)

Paratroops and their parachutes litter the fields of Normandy. (USAF)

C-47s towing Horsa gliders to Normandy. (USAF)

Three Horsa gliders in a field in Normandy after disgorging troops.

USAAF Waco gliders in a French field.

Horsa glider R15 in a pasture.

Opposite page: Horsa gliders and parachutes strewn across fields in France.

RAF Mitchell bombers of 2nd Tactical Air Force with distinctive D-Day invasion stripes on the wing and fuselage fly over a convoy bound for Normandy.

Brigadier the Lord Lovat DSO MC commanded 1st Special Service Brigade composed of four Army, and one Royal Marines Commando. They were given the task of relieving British paratroops at Pegasus Bridge. Lovat is pictured here just after the failed Dieppe Operation.

British 1st Air Service Brigade boarding their vessels on the Hamble River.

Pipe Major William Haskin 'Bill' Millin, plays the pipes for the men of the 1st Air Service Brigade on a football pitch in England.

Piper Bill Millin on LCI (5)519 which ferried Lord Lovat's commandoes onto 'Sword' beach on D-Day. Lovat can be seen in the water third from left.

A British Red Cross jeep crosses Pegasus Bridge.

British troops march across Pegasus Bridge.

Chapter 2

The Advance on Pegasus Bridge

by Pipe Major Bill Millin[9]

'Suddenly the air was split by a piercing sound of bagpipes. Along the beach, some hundred yards away, a piper was marching up and down. There was Piper Bill Millin filling his bag up and getting his wind. Lord Lovat had asked him to play a few tunes. Lord Lovat came up behind Bill, formed up his troops and they marched off in parade-ground style, straight up into the village of Colleville. It was amazing. How could he have the pipes on the beach amidst all this battle noise? Shells screaming and fire all around. And silently, as the sound of the pipes died away into the hinterland of the beach, we got back to work bringing the landing craft in. That was a real high point in the whole landing.

Able Seaman Ken Oakley Royal Navy, Beachmaster's bodyguard, 'F' Commando.

'On the 2nd June the 1st Commando Brigade moved into the concentration areas on the Common, a large area of grassland and trees situated on the main avenue leading out of Southampton. This was to be our home, under canvas and behind barbed wire, until it was time to go aboard the landing craft and take part in the invasion of France. Also in the camp were other allied troops of many nationalities, American, French, Polish, Dutch, Belgians and probably many others. I knew the Southampton area very well. My sister lived here, she was married to a CSM in the Royal Artillery and she had a house about ten minutes' walk from the common. The troops in the camp were not allowed to mix with the general public, so I was hoping that the word would get around that Lord Lovat's commandos were in the area and she would seek me out. I had spent several leaves at her house and had even attended the local dances in the area, accompanied by a girlfriend.

'To prevent boredom and keep everyone occupied, there were cinema shows, football matches, meetings and pep talks about the coming invasion, the showing of maps and models of the French coastline, that no one really understood. When someone asked a question like, 'But where exactly is the landing area?' The answer from the officer would be 'Ah; that is the secret of the moment!'

'I moved around the commando units playing the bagpipes, but fully understanding that one could not inflict bagpipes on anyone if they did not particularly like the instrument. Fortunately, the majority of the troops in the 1st Commando Brigade liked bagpipe music and always gave me a polite welcome whenever I paid them a visit. At times I suspected that they were being polite, as I was the Brigade Piper and also Lovat's personal

---

9   William Haskin Millin, 1st Special Service Brigade.

Piper. Lovat was very popular with each commando unit, particularly 4 Commando and especially 4 Commando (French Troop). Everyone liked Lord Lovat, although we all thought that at 32 he was bit too old for the kind of daredevilry he enjoyed. (I was 21). He was a typical aristocrat who would walk calmly with his head held high while all the rest of us would be ducking and diving to avoid shells. Everyone regarded him as crazy and in retrospect I suppose they thought that I was pretty crazy, too. I had a special relationship with him. He always called me Bill, although it would have been form to use surnames. From late 1942 to May 1944 I had been in a commando training centre, Achnacarry in the Highlands, helping to teach landing techniques to Belgians, Dutch and Americans.[10] We were all volunteers looking for something different and exciting. One day in May 1944 he told me he was forming his own commando brigade and would like me to join and play the pipes. At that time the War Office had banned pipers in action. Lovat told me he was not bothered about the War Office and that I would be the only piper playing at Normandy.[11] I took it as an honour and was quite happy to get away from the training centre.'

'An American soldier was very curious about my role in the coming invasion. 'Piper, what weapons do you carry in action?'

'Just the bagpipes,' I replied.

'He scratched his head and exclaimed, 'Christ, Piper, you sure are in for a hot time if the Germans don't like bagpipes!'

'The highlights of each day were the route marches out of camp and around the outskirts of Southampton and usually a visit to the waterworks, where we would sit by the side of the road, have a refreshment and then march back to camp. In the morning I would play the bagpipes for 45 Royal Marine Commando, marching out of camp playing *Highland Laddie* (a Jacobite song) along the avenue and out into the countryside, the local population stopping to have a look as we passed by. I was hoping that Olive, my sister, would soon get the message and contact me.

'I did not have long to wait. I was piping the Marines back to camp after the route march. We were marching along the avenue striding it out to *Blue Bonnets over the Border* when I saw two figures at the side of the road, jumping up and down and waving to attract my attention. They were Olive, my sister and my ex-girlfriend, Mary. I almost choked on the blow stick when they started to walk alongside me. I looked round at the Royal Marine commando officer. He indicated that he intended to turn into Camp at the first entrance on the left. I turned left and stopped at the entrance to the camp as the commandos swung past me to the tune of *Highland Laddie*. I stopped playing when they disappeared round the first corner inside the camp. Olive and Mary did not have much time for pleasantries with me as the Regimental Police on duty at the gate were soon on the spot and hustled

10 Lovat had taken part in the ill-fated Dieppe operation of August 1942 when 6,100 men, the vast majority of them Canadian, took part. Only 2,500 returned.
11 Pipe Major Jock Slattery played *Blue Bonnets Over the Border* as he led the 1st King's Own Scottish Borderers (9th Brigade, 3rd Division) into battle. *'Gold' 'Juno' 'Sword'* by Georges Bernage (Heimdal 2003).

them on their way, but not before I had a few kisses and a message passed to my relatives in Fort William and Glasgow. I particularly enjoyed my trips out of camp with 4 Commando (French Troop). At first they had difficulty marching in step to the pipes, but later as I quickened the pace to suit their style of marching, they soon got into the swing of it. I was returning from a route march one day with 3 Commando and as we approached the first entrance to the camp on the left, I looked around at the officer. He indicated that the troop would enter the camp at the second entrance. I continued playing the *Nut Brown Maiden* but, unknown to be, the officer turned the 3 Commando into camp at the first entrance and I was left on my own, piping merrily along the main thoroughfare of Southampton, oblivious to what was going on behind me. I was quite happy, the pipes were going well; the civilians passing me by had smiles on their faces. Everything looked great. 'That evening a rumour spread round the camp that we would be leaving soon for the embarkation area. Next day 'Shimi' Lovat called a meeting of all ranks for a final briefing. We gathered around him, some sitting on the grass, others just standing about, all of us without exception very keen to know what was going on and when we would be leaving the camp. Lovat addressed the gathering first in English and then in French.

'I... took two minutes. It was simple enough, the message plain. I weighed each word and then drove it home. I concentrated on the task ahead and simple facts - how to pace the battle.'

First he spoke in English and then to the Free French commandos who were joining the exercise in colloquial French '*Vous allez rentrer chez vous. Vous serez les premiers militaires francais en uniforme cl casser la gueule des salauds en France merne. A chacun son Boche.*' Lovat reminded his own commandos that 'they knew their job and I knew that they would not fail... it appeared a tough assignment, but we held the advantage both in initiative and fire power... it was better to attack than to defend... The brigade was going to make history,' he said; he had 'complete confidence in every man taking part!' Lovat ended 'this harangue' with the suggestion that 'if you wish to live to a ripe old age - keep moving tomorrow. And so we stood across the sea to France... [12]

'We would be packing up and leaving this afternoon. Our job, after securing the coastal area, was to get to the bridges near the village of Bénouville on the Caen Canal and River Orne where airborne troops had already landed. He continued, 'I wish you all the very best of luck in what lies ahead: this will be the greatest military venture of all time and the Commando Brigade has an important role to play.' We would lead the assault force going ashore and we should be proud to be taking such an

---

12 See: *D-Day: Those Who Were There* by Juliet Gardiner (Collins & Brown 1994). On Sunday at a religious service the padre warned his 'congregation' to expect grisly wounds. 'It's God's business' the padre said 'and if it wasn't, I wouldn't touch it with a bargepole.' Doon Campbell said that the men's mood was 'awful'. Lovat interrupted the service and finished the sermon himself, later telling the padre that he had damaged the men's morale. Next day Campbell was returning to his tent when he heard a shot ring out. The padre had committed suicide. *D-Day 6.6.44* by Dan Perry (BBC Books 2004).

important part in the invasion. 'A hundred years from now your children's children will say, 'They must have been giants in those days'.

'I went round the camp that afternoon and shook hands with all the friends I had made during our short stay in the concentration area. Everyone was very friendly, even the officer who could not stand the sound of bagpipes and got very annoyed when I passed by his tent at 06.30 playing Reveille. He would come out of his tent in his shirt-tail and shake his fist at me, shouting, 'you noisy bastard, why don't you keep to the other side of the camp?' That afternoon he arrived at my tent, a large smile on his face and his hand outstretched. He shook me warmly by the hand and said, 'Best of luck, Piper. Sorry to see you go. We shall miss you and your bagpipes tomorrow morning.' As a member of the permanent staff he would be staying on at the camp and no doubt was pleased to be seeing the back of me and the pipes.

'Having finished packing our rucksacks, we made our way to the camp exits and clambered aboard the waiting transports and were soon on our way along roads crammed with military vehicles of all descriptions. Heavy and light tanks, SP guns and dozens of military troop carriers. Military Police were constantly moving up and down the convoy sorting out the many traffic jams. Now and again we passed groups of civilians standing at street corners and at the side of the road. There were a few cheers here and there along the route, but most of the onlookers just stood and stared. Some of the commandos were waving to the groups of people, but most appeared to be silent and thoughtful.

'As I looked out from the back of the transport I could now recognise the countryside. There was the Hamble River up ahead and now coming into view the 'Rising Sun' pub that I had visited several times two years ago with a girlfriend, when I was on leave in the area. Now the circumstances were very different. A few minutes later we passed the pub, turned left alongside the river, along a narrow road and into a field, where the transports stopped. This was to be our embarkation area for the invasion of France. We all tumbled out of the transports and, on looking around; I could see that we were about two hundred yards from the 'Rising Sun'. It might be possible to slip away later for a glass of beer! On one side of the field was the Hamble River and tied up at a long jetty were many landing-craft, one behind the other, as far as the eye could see. The craft looked very small. Surely these were not the landing-craft that would be taking us across the Channel? I am not a very good sailor and could not help thinking about what lay ahead if the weather was rough.

'The men of the Commando Brigade sat about the field in small groups surrounded by their equipment. Some played cards, others passed the time waving to girls leaning out of a window of a house a short distance away. The girls appeared to be dressed in Wrens' uniforms. The house was probably a Naval HQ. The girls were waving back to the commandos and there was a lot of laughing and joking going on. Other commandos were playing a game of football. It was a pleasant summer evening and just beginning to get dusk. I was just contemplating whether it was possible to slip away and treat myself to a pint of the best bitter at the 'Rising Sun' when someone shouted from across the field, 'What about a tune, Piper?'

'Why not?' I thought. 'The pub is probably closed anyway.'

'I placed the pipes on my shoulder, blew them up and strolled off around the field visiting the various groups of commandos and playing a request here and there. The pipes were sounding very well and I felt that I could play for hours. The whole scene in front of me could have been of a large party of Boy Scouts preparing to go off to camp. The only difference being the presence of so much battle equipment and weapons. The Press were moving about the field taking photographs and appeared to be interviewing some of the commandos.

'I stopped playing as someone indicated to me that we were now preparing to go aboard the landing-craft. 'Well, this is it,' I thought, as I slung my rucksack on my shoulder, tucked the bagpipes under the other arm and made off across the field towards the landing-craft. I looked at the weapons being carried by my comrades; rifles, grenades, automatic weapons, mortars, all the paraphernalia of war. Looking at the bagpipes I was carrying, I thought, 'Let's hope the Germans like bagpipe music.' I looked around for Lovat. He noticed me first. 'Come on, Piper; get aboard the leading-craft!' Once on board I went below and deposited my rucksack in what appeared to be very cramped conditions indeed. Returning on deck with my bagpipes, I looked around for Shimi Lovat. He was probably wanting me to play him a Highland air. He was on the bridge in conversation with the Naval Officer commanding the flotilla of landing-craft.

'Lovat and I went on the first boat, LCI(S) 519 and would lead the flotilla of 21 small infantry landing crafts down river, past the Isle of Wight and out into the English Channel. Sure enough, someone approached me and said that the Brigadier would like me to play a tune as we moved down river. I looked up at the bridge where Lovat was standing; he nodded his head, so I made my way to the front of the landing-craft.

'We were moving slowly as I started to play *The Road to The Isles*. I felt excited, but also with a certain amount of apprehension about the journey. The Isle of Wight lay ahead and to the right. Looking around I could see hundreds of ships, a huge armada of large and small ships, all kinds of warships and dozens of various kinds of landing craft. What a wonderful sight it was, as we passed these vessels all queuing up to take their turn in line. I was now playing the *Skye Boat Song*. Someone managed to broadcast the piping over the loudhailer system. This brought a terrific response from the invasion fleet. Troops on board the transports were throwing their hats into the air and cheering. At this moment I was feeling very proud that the Commando Brigade was at the forefront of the invasion. Brigadier Lord Lovat, 1st Special Service Brigade, said, 'You are going to lead the biggest invasion in the history of warfare.'

'Thanks very much,' was my immediate thought but though I could have refused, there was something in the way he put it that made me feel I had already volunteered. 'Just think if I had turned the brigadier down. I might have ended up in the cookhouse and then I would have missed out on the most memorable experience of my life.

'The sea was now getting a bit choppy and a biting wind was blowing across the deck. I stopped playing as it was very difficult standing upright. We were now out into the Channel and well past the Isle of Wight. Time to put the bagpipes away. As I made my way across the deck to get below, the small craft was pitching and rolling and slapping down onto the waves. I reached the hatchway with difficulty and went below.

'They were all packed in like sardines. The air was thick with cigarette and cigar smoke. Someone was spewing his guts up in the small door less toilet. He was lying face down on the floor retching away for all he was worth. Several others were watching him intently, their faces a strange blue/green colour. The smell of sick was now added to the smell of cigarette and cigars and before the night is over there will no doubt be other smells.

'I descended into this very overcrowded area. There was a choice. I could stay here with all the smells, or go back on deck with the biting wind and the cold. I decided to stay below deck, no matter what.

'There was a space next to four card players. They moved reluctantly as I squeezed in beside them. They were hunched over, intent on their game, the pennies clinking into a Green Beret from time to time. Two commandos were checking their weapons; others were curled up trying to sleep. The sick man was now joined by those with the blue/green faces who had been watching him so intently and the smell of sick was now almost overpowering.

'The craft continued to roll alarmingly, crashing down from time to time with a force that shook it from stem to stern. It was now only a matter of time and a very short time at that, before I joined the sick people lying with their heads in the toilet and spewing all over the floor. I dozed off, must have been for only a few minutes. I awoke feeling seasick. The card players were still at it, the pennies still clinking into the Green Beret. A commando was reading a cowboy paperback novel and laughing away to himself. The sick men were still in the toilet, one of them was shouting, 'Why doesn't this fucking boat sink and put us out of our misery?'

'I made my way over the sprawling bodies as quickly as possible in the direction of the toilet. Just in time, with not a moment to lose and added my pennyworth to what had accumulated since passing the Isle of Wight. After a few more visits to the toilet I must have drifted off to sleep again. When I awoke I looked at my watch. It was just after 4 am. The craft was still rolling but not as much as in the earlier part of the night. The engines were not so noisy and I had a feeling that we must be near the French coast. I stretched out as best I could and stared at the bulkhead. I looked at one of the card players. He was a married man and had shown me a picture of his wife when we were at the camp in Southampton. He did not look concerned about anything other than the card game. I was glad I was not married. I would probably worry about her worrying about me. I looked at my watch again and decided to go on deck. Pulling on my jacket I made my way across the sleeping bodies to the steps leading to the hatchway and arrived on deck. The craft was rolling from side to side; the sea was white and rough, accompanied by a very strong wind blowing across the bows. 'Christ, its cold,' I thought, as I shivered in the entrance to the hatchway. The rails of the craft were down ready for action and as I gazed at the scene I thought, 'It's bad out here on deck, but a lot worse in the smelly conditions below.' The cold wind blowing on my face helped to revive me and I was feeling a little better. As I held on to the door of the hatchway, I muttered to myself, 'For Christ's sake! I don't care how many Germans are waiting for us, or what the conditions are on the French beaches, the sooner we get off this bloody craft the better.'

'I stared ahead and now could make out the outline of the French coast. Moving out from the shelter of the hatchway I lay face down on the metal deck and held on to a large iron ring to prevent myself from being swept overboard. There was no one else in sight!

'Where is the crew?' I turned round and looked at the bridge. The commander and Shimi Lovat were looking towards the French coast through binoculars. I had another look at the coastline; further details were now visible, bombed and damaged houses along the sea front.

'I made my way quickly below, pulled on my rucksack, picked up the bagpipes and noticed that the other commandos were getting themselves ready. No one was saying a word; even the very sick people of a few hours ago were silently getting their equipment together.

'As we assembled on deck, the craft was still pitching and rolling, but a little steadier than previously.

'Warships of the Allied fleet were firing their guns at targets ashore. Some of the salvoes were passing overhead with a loud roar. There was now a lot of activity. Commandos were assembling in file at the front of the craft, close to the ramps. The crew were dashing about getting things ready. I went to the rear of the craft to deposit my bagpipe box. It would be too much to carry once ashore. The naval officer had now gathered his crew together and was shaking hands with each one, wishing them luck.

'Do you mind if I leave this box here, Sir?' I said, addressing the Officer. He looked me up and down for a few seconds as if to say, 'Do what you like with the bloody box!'

'I joined the other commandos at the front of the craft. The German gunners were now joining in. Their fire was very accurate and large spouts of water were shooting up around the landing-craft. To our right a landing-craft had received a direct hit and was burning fiercely. The occupants were scrambling into the water. No one seemed to mind the noise of the salvoes passing overhead, or the fate of the unfortunate occupants of the landing-craft that had been hit. Everyone was staring ahead as the landing-craft drew closer to the beaches. I could see the coast very clearly now. Two tanks at the water's edge were on fire and a large cloud of black smoke was blowing across the dunes. It appeared that the tanks had been knocked out before they had even got as far as the dunes.

'As I watched the scene in front of me another salvo of shells from the warships passed overhead and hit a house on the sea front, throwing large chunks of masonry high into the air. There was a constant whine of bullets or shrapnel close by. We were now preparing to go ashore and I was standing behind Shimi Lovat at the left ramp. The commandos were now jumping into the water. One of the card players on the sea journey from England, the married man, was hit in the face by a piece of shrapnel as he stepped onto the ramp. He clung on to the ramp for a few seconds and then toppled into the sea.

'There appeared to be about one hundred yards of water between us and the beach. Lovat was off the craft and wading towards the beach. I jumped off the ramp as quickly as possible, holding the bagpipes above my head and landed in water up to my waist. I felt myself falling backwards due to the weight of my rucksack. Luckily someone pulled me upright and I struggled through the water still holding the pipes above my head. I could see Shimi Lovat just ahead of me, I was catching him up.

'The water was now at knee level and the beach was just a few yards away. There was a lot of noise, the sound of automatic fire and what appeared to be mortar shells bursting on the beach away to the right. I placed the bagpipes on my shoulder, blew them up and started to play *Highland Laddie* as I waded the few yards to the beach. Lovat turned his head towards me when he heard the pipes. He looked at me for a moment, appeared to smile and then continued on his way.
'The sound of explosions and the whine of bullets seemed very much closer, even above the drone of the pipes, as I now stepped onto the beach'.

'My mind concentrated on finding a path through the underwater obstructions. Fortunately at that state of the tide, the tops of many of them were still visible sprouting above the surface of the sea, many with lethal attachments. Working completely by instinct ... I felt I could discern a clear path through the menacing stakes. It looked a bit of a zigzag but I backed my instinct and took 519 through with rapid helm orders. We emerged unscathed and I called for more power from the engine room to thrust our bows hard on to the beach to ensure as dry a landing as possible. Then we kept both engines running at half ahead to hold the bows in position. At that moment we were hit by armour-piercing shells which zipped through the port Oerlikon gun shield but fortunately missed both gunners and our commandos. 502 (Lieutenant John Seymour RANVR) carrying the remainder of Brigade Headquarters, beached very close on our port hand and as she did so she was hit by armour-piercing shells which penetrated four petrol tanks and hit the port engine and put it out of action. Perhaps I should explain that each of our craft carried 4,000 gallons of high octane petrol in non-sealing tanks just abaft the bridge. Had the enemy used incendiary or high explosive ammunition 502 would have blown up and disintegrated in a sheet of flame which would have engulfed them and us in 519. The Brigade would almost certainly have lost its trusted leader, Lord Lovat and most of the Headquarters group. At the end of the day I estimated that half of the Brigade might not have got ashore but for the fact that the Germans used solid shot on us, which was really meant for tanks.

I gave the order for our troops to land. The ramps were manhandled over the bows by our well trained ramp crew under Sub-Lieutenant Stephen Garrett RNVR and our commandos began to land in about three feet of water as calmly as though on exercise. Each man carried some 80lb of weaponry and gear and clambering down our narrow landing bows on to a danger-laden strip of sand could have been no fun. We bade goodbye to Lord Lovat and wished him good luck... as pipes gave heart and encouragement to all. Then we began the tricky task of coming off the beach stem first through the obstructions to make way for our second wave of LCI(S) to come in to land 3 Commando and 45 Commando Royal Marines.'

Lieutenant Commander Rupert Curtis RNVR Commander LCI (5)519 which ferried Lord Lovat's commandos ashore onto 'Sword' beach.

'D-Day was to be my eighth landing with 3 Commando, but I was most unhappy about it for it was to be my first in daylight and the first time we were not to be first in. We were in the second flight and due to land after the hornet's nest had been disturbed. When ordered below for the run-in, I was sitting in the forward space on the port side. The next thing I remember is coming to with my head just above the water which had flooded the compartment. The craft had a terrible list and the space was littered with bodies and flotsam. The water was cold and bloodstained.

'I saw a hatchway some feet away. I struggled to my feet, but found it almost impossible, for I was still wearing my special combat waistcoat, which was packed with ammunition, explosive charges and two 3-inch mortar shells, which every man had to carry. As I tried to get to my feet, I must have impacted what transpired to be a bad fracture of both tibia and fibula above my left ankle. As I struggled to un-strap my waistcoat, a crew member looked down through the hatch way I had seen and lowered a rope which I tied round my waist. With another crew member, he pulled me to the deck.

'We were told we had been hit badly, were sinking, but another craft was alongside. I was strapped into a stretcher, made of split cane and canvas, like a mummy, from shoulders to ankles, 'with my arms inside. I was carried to another LCI(S) lurching alongside. My end had come, or so I thought, when I landed on the other craft, for I seemed just to roll across the deck. I was carried, laid beside the bridge and told not to worry as we were returning immediately to Blighty. I heard an almighty crash and was told that the engine room had been hit and the craft was being abandoned.

'The second transfer was to a floating tank. I was laid across the turret in my wrapper, with the tank commander holding me in position. On the beach I was laid in the tracks of a tank or similar vehicle, where I lay petrified for most of the day thinking that other tanks would grind me into the beach. The medics eventually found me.

Private Kenneth Holmes, 3 Commando, who was evacuated to England.

'As we hit the beach, I went forrard to see if the brows had been shot over their rollers. The party of seamen - four or six - were a mass of duffel-coats, steel helmets, teeth, jaws, brains and blood. There was a sweet sickly smell, stronger than all the cordite, grease and oil normally present in almost any small craft in action. I saw a rope trailing into the sea. Shouting 'Follow me', I swung myself over the side into what I expected to be three or four feet of water. In my panic, I had not ensured that the rope was made fast inboard; the loose end snaked across the deck as I; gripping the rope, neatly dropped like a plummet into a six-foot shell hole which the tide had covered. I was well and truly stuck in the sands of Normandy with eighteen inches of water over my head.

'Help was quickly forthcoming. An RAMC medical orderly waded into the water and dragged me ashore to the cheers of those on board the craft who had the sense to make their exit in a more dignified way. Wading to the water's edge, I could not help noticing the number of battle-dressed bodies, all face down, gently floating on the tide line surrounded by a pinkish tinge. The sound of the Adjutant's hunting horn made me gather my wits, impressing on me the need to make for the commando RV.'

19-year old Lieutenant Alex Sudborough, 45 (Royal Marine) Commando.

'I was not really frightened...' continues Bill Millin '...because we had practiced landings so many times before but this time we were being fired on. Shells were bursting in the water. There were bodies floating in the water and lying across the beach. Two tanks were burning fiercely. It was pure noise and confusion. Commandos were rushing past me and up the beach. I stopped playing the pipes as I passed between two dead soldiers lying at the water's edge, one with half of his face blown away. They were moving back and forward with the surf. Through my mind flashed the instructions we had been given at our last briefing in England. 'Get off the beach as quickly as possible.'

'There were several commandos crouching behind a low wall sheltering from the enemy fire. Several wounded were sitting with their backs to the wall, their faces a strange grey colour. It was a bizarre experience to walk out of the water still playing and to be confronted with the sight of wounded British soldiers lying where they had fallen. Other commandos were attempting to dig in. It appeared to me that we were being pinned down on the beach! I looked around for Lovat and spotted him a short distance away on the dunes talking to someone. I moved quickly in the direction of a narrow road that led off the beach. As I approached the road I noticed at its entrance eight, or maybe ten commandos and they all appeared to be wounded. They had possibly been cut down by machine-gun or mortar fire as they attempted to advance from the beach. They were shocked to see me in my kilt and playing the bagpipes. Two of them called out to me as I approached. Jock, for Christ's sake! Where are the medics?' They repeated this several times above the noise. I had no idea, but I shouted to them that they were on their way. I knelt down beside one of the wounded and was attempting to drag him to the safety of the wall when a long burst of machine-gun fire came down the road. I scrambled very quickly to the cover of a doorway and pressed my back against it as close as I possibly could.

'I stood there gazing at the wounded lying in the sand in front of me. One of them was still calling for help. Suddenly there was a clanking sound to my right. Looking round I could see a flail tank coming up the beach from the water's edge and heading in the direction of the road. Its chains were thumping the ground in front of it as it approached. As the tank drew closer I could see the commander's head looking out from the turret. As the tank came rumbling on I thought, 'Christ! It's too wide to get up this road' and if it did make the attempt I would be crushed against the wall! I scrambled out from the doorway and out of the path of the tank. The firing was still coming from the German position at the top of the road. I tried to attract the attention of the tank Commander by pointing to the wounded in his path. He appeared not to notice and the tank rumbled closer and closer, eventually churning up the wounded lying in its path, its front gun blasting away at the German position at the top of the road. As it disappeared up the road crushing the walls on either side, I look briefly at the mangled bodies of the soldiers and dashed along the beach to join the other commandos and Lovat. It was very traumatic watching those men die. It was horrifying. I felt so helpless.

'The beach was still under fire from the German guns, plus the salvoes from the Allied warships out at sea were crashing into a spot just off the beach. The two tanks were still burning fiercely, the black smoke blowing across the dunes.

'I joined Lovat as the Brigade Major was telling him that a message had just come through that the Airborne Forces who had landed during the night had captured the bridges over the River Orne and the canal. This was good news for us, as we could now cross the Orne by the bridges rather than having to swim across.

'The bridges were a long way from the beach and a lot was to happen before we reached the Orne. The Brigade Major interrupted his conversation with Lovat and looking at me as if he had just noticed me, remarked, 'Piper, how about a tune?'

'What tune would you like, Sir?' I asked.

'He thought for a moment and then said, 'Play *The Road to the Isles.'*
'Would you prefer me to walk up and down the beach, Sir?'
'Yes, that would be fine,' he replied. I placed the pipes on my shoulder and started off at a fairly brisk pace and at the water's edge. I had hardly gone fifty yards when I heard a bellowing in my left ear, 'what are you fucking well playing at, Piper? You mad bastard! Don't you think there's enough going on here without you attracting every fucking German in France?' It was a commando sergeant and it was obvious from the look on his face that he did not like bagpipes, at least not here on a Normandy beach. I continued playing as he stomped off glaring back at me. Other commandos at the top of the dunes were giving me the victory sign and waving to me. I passed the two dead commandos lying in the surf, their bodies moving back and forth, as the water lapped on to the beach. Troops were still coming ashore

from the landing craft, most of them passing me by without a second glance. I stopped playing when I noticed that Lovat, the Brigade Major and the rest of the commandos had disappeared off the beach. I doubled across the sand dunes and caught up with them, as they were crossing a field.

'We were now heading inland, crossing a couple of minefields marked, *Achtung! Minen*. Probably the German troops had no time to take down their warning signs when we arrived suddenly from the sea.

'There was still automatic fire close at hand. It appeared to be coming from somewhere to our left and at the front of the column. Everyone got down in the grass. I rolled over onto my back, my rucksack propping me up. I gazed up at the sky. It was a lovely morning. The sky was blue and I could hear a bird singing. Everything seemed peaceful, except for the rattle of the automatic fire away on our left.

'As I continued to stare upwards, I was surprised to see what looked like mortar bombs! They were flying in formation and heading in the direction of the beach, a few hundred yards to our rear. A few seconds later they exploded, with a crump, crump, crump. Other bombs were now coming over, also in formation. As they descended they let out a loud screaming noise that was quite frightening. This was our first introduction to the German multi-barrelled mortar. Its bombs exploded with a loud roar, followed by thick black smoke. The Germans certainly had the range on the beach and the troops coming ashore at this moment were getting a hot reception.

'We were on the move again, across a few more minefields, then onto a road. There was a rifle shot close by, then another shot. The commando, who had been reading the cowboy paper-back on the landing-craft yesterday evening on our way across the Channel, was hit in the chest. He fell forward onto the grass verge at the side of the road. Someone turned him over onto his back; his face had the deadly pallor all soldiers have when they have been wounded. A medic was opening his battledress blouse as we moved on. We wondered where the next shot was coming from.

'The further we moved inland the more frequent and active were the enemy snipers. The sound of the guns and the bombardment at the landing beaches was becoming fainter.

'We entered a small village [Saint-Aubin-d'Arquenay] and to my surprise there were quite a few people about. They stood at the side of the road and waved, some shouted, 'Anglais, Anglais'. I was playing *Rawentree* (The Scot's sacred tree that drives out evil spirits) and this brought on a round of handclapping from the villagers. Two nuns were handing out glasses of wine to the commandos. A group of commandos on the other side of the road and about fifty yards ahead of me had stopped and were firing their weapons at a house a few yards in front of the column. I stopped playing the pipes as some civilians rushed past me trying to get to the rear and out of the way of the shooting. There was someone in the house firing an automatic weapon at us. A commando was lying face down in the gutter. He was levelling a PIAT gun at the house. He fired and the bomb hit the house dead centre, above the front door. The blast completely destroyed the building and threw rubble and clouds of smoke and dust into the air.

'As we moved on through the village I could hear rifle shots coming from our rear; no doubt other members of the Brigade were having problems.

'I was now at the head of the column as we left the built-up area and headed along the road towards the village of Bénouville. The road in front was fairly straight with trees along both sides. On the right were cornfields and on the left the fields sloped away to the Orne Canal.

'I was playing *Highland Laddie* as I marched along at the head of the column, single file on either side of the road. I looked round from time to time, Lovat was immediately behind me and the remainder strung out along the road to the rear.

'Suddenly two shots rang out in quick succession. I could hear them very clearly, even above the sound of the pipes. I looked ahead and could see the sniper in a tree on the right side of the road. Another shot rang out, he was clearly visible now. Looking round I could see some of the commandos were taking cover at the side of the road. Others were firing their weapons at the sniper in the tree. I stopped playing and looked towards the tree. The sniper scrambled down from the branches and then ran into the cornfield; his head bobbing up and down through the corn, a barrage of rifle shots followed him. Lovat, I could see, was taking a few pot-shots himself at the running figure.

'Two commandos went into the field and brought out the sniper's body and dumped it at the side of the road. As I looked down at the body, I wondered why he had not shot at me, an obvious target. Lovat asked me to keep playing the bagpipes as long as possible as we were now approaching the area where the Airborne Forces had captured the bridges over the Orne.

'I placed the bagpipes on my shoulder and started to play a well known Scottish tune called *Lochan Side*, keeping up a brisk pace on the road to Bénouville. As we approached the village I could hear the sound of heavy firing, mortars and automatic weapons. The Orne Canal was flowing parallel to the road, so the bridges could not be far off. Suddenly about fifty yards ahead of me a group of figures appeared running towards us, their hands held high above their heads. As they drew level with us they looked scared stiff. These were the first Germans I had seen with their hands up.

'They were hustled unceremoniously to the rear. I continued piping and as we approached Bénouville the road turned right at the entrance to the village and we came under some rifle and automatic fire. I stopped playing the pipes as the road turned right and joined a group of commandos who were crouched behind a low wall on the right-hand side of the road. There were several wounded lying at the side of the road being tended to by a medic. Opposite us, sheltering behind the gable end of a house was another group of commandos. Sitting on the road and leaning back on the grass embankment is Taffy. He looks terrible and appears to be wounded pretty badly. I cannot see the wound; it's probably in his back. He is just lying there staring ahead with glazed eyes. Christ! I shared a bottle of beer with him yesterday; he was talking about his wife all the time'.

'After sailing, below deck we made a very special study of our maps, checked our arms and ammunition and had plenty of hot soup provided by one of the crew. June the 6th, soon after dawn, we were crouching low on the deck and to our left a battleship was firing and above a few Spitfires to cover us in. At this point the enemy gunners were trying to get our range and shells were bursting all around us. Soon we were heading for our part of the Normandy coast and at once all hell seemed to break out. As the enemy machine gunners opened up, very calmly the LCI crew dropped the landing ramps down and with good luck from the crew we started on our way through the sea. Part of our task was to reach the airborne forces who in the night had taken and were holding the bridge, now named Pegasus Bridge. After leaving the beach we made our way through open grassland and all around the Germans had placed notice boards warning of mines. But by a careful study of the ground we found the way across a part where cattle had been grazing some days before. We moved so fast that we were on to one group of Germans drinking coffee in the edge of a field. Our instructions had to be carried out. Push on to the bridge, never mind the odds.'

W. H. Jeffries, 6 Commando.

'I moved along the low wall crouching down and holding the bagpipes to my chest' continues Bill Millin - 'With the group of commandos sheltering behind the gable end of the house opposite was the CO of 6 Commando, Colonel Derek Mills-Roberts, a veteran of Dieppe. On the beach he had remarked conversationally to a corporal: 'Seems ages since we had a dry landing. D'you find the sea cold?' He looked impatient and kept peering round the building and into the village. Suddenly a light tank appeared and turned into the village. Mills-Roberts got his eye on me and shouted 'Right, Piper, behind the tank.' I struck up the pipes and commenced playing *Blue Bonnets over the Border* and moving quickly behind the tank, the others following close behind. The tank stopped in the centre of the village, opposite the church and started to fire its gun at the belfry. Lovat was also firing his rifle at something that had attracted his attention in the churchyard. I stopped the pipes and looked at the spire of the church. There was a large hole on the left side and it looked as if it had been hit by a shell. There was the sound of automatic fire from inside and three commandos emerged with a wounded German. Across the road a few commandos were firing their weapons through the windows of a house and another commando was throwing a hand-grenade into a garden at the side of the house.

'We continued through the village. Looking back, I noticed that the tank had disappeared as mysteriously as it had appeared and that was the last I was to see of it. The crew of the tank were probably just as pleased to see us as we were to see them. A tank on its own without infantry support, I suppose, feels very vulnerable. It certainly helped us get into the village.

'We are now at the far end of the village and looking out onto the road leading to the Orne bridges. There is a haze and clouds of dust everywhere. It seems unreal as I stand at the exit from the village waiting for Lovat to come along. The houses, the few French people, who looked scared stiff, even my commando friends look different; their faces appear set and tense. Some look fierce, others appear to look straight through me. They probably think the same about me. I have had no conversation with anyone other than a signal of recognition since leaving the Hamble River yesterday evening, 5th June.

'Lovat approaches me. 'Piper, we are leaving here now and I want you to play your pipes as long as you possibly can. The Orne bridges are not far off and I would like the Forces holding the bridges to know when they hear the bagpipes that the Commando Brigade is close at hand.'

'As I started up the bagpipes and headed out along the road playing Blue Bonnets over the Border and keeping well into the side of the road, with Lovat and the others close behind, I could hear the sound of heavy firing in the distance and the now familiar crump of the mortars. We continued round a bend in the road and I could now see a large house up ahead. The house was about three-hundred yards away and our route veered to the left in front of it. I was fascinated with the house. It had a low wall round it, with iron railings on top. The door was in the centre, with large windows on either side. I found myself, as I was walking along playing the bagpipes, looking mainly at the windows for the presence of snipers.

'Above the sound of the pipes I could hear the rattle of automatic fire. Glancing round, Lovat was still there, the rest of the commandos strung out on either side of the road. Everything seemed to be all right.

'About one-hundred yards from the house I could see figures sitting about on the grass at the side of the road, as it veered round to the left. I stopped playing and was delighted to recognise the figures as 4 Commando (French Troop). They looked tired but cheerful. I looked along the row of faces and Chauvet, my friend from the Southampton camp days, was there, sitting, back against a grass embankment, drinking from his water bottle.

'I looked at Lovat, he nodded his head and I left the column and went over and shook hands with Chauvet. They had had a very busy morning after the landing at La Brêche. 4 Commando and the French Commando had swung left from the beach and had attacked the coastal town of Ouistreham, capturing the heavily defended casino. They had then made their way across country to link with the rest of the Brigade'.

'Private John Mason of 4 Commando was shocked to find himself 'running through piles of dead infantry who had been knocked down like nine-pins'. Another commando coming in with Lord Lovat's HQ at roughly the same time, recalled seeing bodies' sprawled all over the beach, some with legs, arms and heads missing, the blood clotting the wet sand'. Lance-Corporal C. Morris of the same headquarters recollected: 'Everyone was now sitting very quiet and kept looking at each other and making efforts to smile; but it was all very forced and tense, though we knew that we should be all right once we started to land and have something to occupy our minds.'
Charles Whiting.

'It was clear that the Franco-Britannique Commando had landed at a critical moment. They crossed the beach with utmost dash and determination to force a path through the defence and start the attack by swinging left on to

Ouistreham. In the beach crossing they suffered some forty casualties and would have suffered more if they had not moved with speed. Some men were killed and wounded in the assault craft. Colonel Robert Dawson was wounded on the beach so that his second-in-command Major R. P. Monday, together with Commandant Kieffer, led the gallant drive into Ouistreham to silence the German batteries and over run the Casino strong-point - a task which they carried out successfully after heavy fighting and many losses.'

Lieutenant Commander Rupert Curtis.

Two troops of French Fusiliers Marins and a light machine gun platoon (177 men) under Commandant Philippe Kieffer had landed at 07.55 hours. Kieffer was wounded on the beach and 40 French commandos were killed or wounded. (When Oberstleutnant Josef 'Pips' Priller, Kommodore, Jagdgeschwader 26 'Schlageter' and his regular Kacmarek (wingman), Unteroffizier Heinz Wodarczyk attacked 'Sword' Beach six German prisoners took advantage of the situation and tried to bolt but Kieffer's' men promptly mowed them down.) They headed east to the resort of Riva Bella and the port of Ouistreham at the mouth of the Orne. The Germans had fortified the site of the casino at Riva Bella and it was manned by companies from the 1st/736th Infantry Regiment and the 642nd Ost battalion 716th Static Infantry Division. Told that he would lead the attack on the casino, one sergeant, Comte Guy de Montlaur said to Kieffer: 'It will be a pleasure. I have lost several fortunes in that place.' (The casino building itself was demolished by the Germans in October 1942 and replaced with concreted gun positions which were attacked by a DD tank of the 13th/18th Hussars before the final assault.) The French destroyer *la Combattante* assisted in the bombardment of Ouistreham in support of the attack by the Fusiliers Marins. Kieffer was born in Haiti to a family originating in Alsace and had learned English in the USA. A reserve officer aboard the old battleship *Courbet*[13] in 1940, he had escaped from France with a few soldiers that made up the garrison at Ste-Vaast-la-Hougue on the Cotentin Peninsular and had responded to the appeal to join Colonel Charles de Gaulle's fight against Hitler. Inspired by the raids by British commandos on the Lofoten Islands, Kieffer proposed to the French Naval HQ on Clapham Common that there was potential to raise a French Commando specifically to raid the French coast and the first French Commando unit, 1er Compaignie Fusiler Marin (1st Marine Rifle Company) was finally raised in 1941. The Fusiliers Marins took the casino and the lock gates on the canal suffering heavy losses in the process and Kieffer was twice wounded. It was said that his son was killed fighting for the Resistance shortly before his father entered Paris with the Free French Forces. After the war Philippe Kieffer sat in the French National Assembly.

13 On D-Day *Courbet* was towed across the Channel and sunk off Ouistreham to act as a breakwater for the Mulberry harbour at Arromanches). *la Combattante* was built in 1942 at the Fairfields Yard in Glasgow. On 23 February 1945 she disappeared in the North Sea. Sixty-five French and two Royal Navy sailors were lost. *Major & Mrs Holt's Battlefield Guide: Normandy Landing Beaches* (Leo Cooper, 1999, 2000, 2002).

'I rushed away to catch up with Lovat, who had been striding past the commandos resting on either side of the road,' continues Bill Millin. 'I shouted back at Chauvet: 'Don't forget, you promised to show me the sights of Paris!' He shouted back at me, 'It's a bit early to talk about being a tourist.'

'The Orne Canal Bridge was about two hundred yards or so down the road and I caught up with Lovat at the head of the Brigade. Being an aristocratic type, Lovat just carried on and never ducked down, while I was crawling through ditches. He was talking to an Airborne officer. The bridge was a heavy, riveted sort of structure, with heavy metal sides. The bridge could be lifted to allow shipping to pass through and luckily it was lowered at the moment. A pall of black smoke hung over the scene and there was the sound of rifle and automatic fire. The fire seemed to be coming from German positions somewhere to the right. From where I was standing, almost directly across the road from a cafe next to the bridge, I could hear the bullets hitting off the metal sides. Wounded were being carried into the cafe. The Airborne Officer walked away and Lovat came towards me, indicating that we should now cross over the bridge. I placed the bagpipes on my shoulder and was about to start playing when a voice immediately behind me called out, 'For Christ's sake, Piper, wait until we get to the other side!'

'The pipes remained on my shoulder as I crossed over the bridge with Lovat. There was a lot of noise. I could hear the bullets striking the sides of the bridge and the occasional ricochet of a bullet passing overhead. I glanced round and could see the other commandos behind us. They were crouching low and taking advantage of the protection offered by the metal sides of the bridge.

'As we approached the other side, Lovat went forward to speak to an Airborne Officer and then turned to me, with what I thought was a look of consternation on his face and motioned impatiently for me to start playing the pipes. 'Right Piper, keep playing your bagpipes from here, along the road and across the next bridge.' I started off along the road playing the *March of the Cameron Men,* not very appropriate as 'Shimi' Lovat was Chief of the Clan Fraser! The weight of my rucksack was beginning to affect my playing. After all, the beach was a long way back and I had been playing the bagpipes most of the way'.

'A little after mid-day now and then sweet music on the air - bagpipes! A company of commandos, with a piper at the head and their officer next wearing a white pullover, had reached us from the beach. What a joy for us all - temporarily, for as they crossed some of the lads were hit by the snipers. We buried one by the bridge next day. I painted Lieutenant Campbell's name on an improvised cross using a tin of paint and a brush from the café by the bridge.'
Sapper Cyril Larkin.

The road ahead was dusty and through the dust Bill Millin could see another bridge looming up ahead of him. 'The distance between the two bridges was I suppose about two-hundred yards. As I drew closer I could see that it was narrower than the bridge we had just crossed and there were no metal sides to give us cover as we crossed over. About fifty yards from the bridge I could see straight across to the other side. There were two paratroopers dug in and they were both indicating to us not to cross, as the bridge was under fire. They were pointing to the river banks on our right and possibly warning us about the presence of snipers.

'I was now playing *Blue Bonnets over the Border,* as I looked round for Lovat. He was strolling along at the head of the column as if he were out for a walk round his estate in Scotland. He indicated with his hands for me to proceed across to the other side. As I stepped onto the bridge still playing *Blue Bonnets over the Border* I kept my eyes fixed on the two Paratroopers in the slit trench on the far side. Both were firing their weapons at targets on the river banks. I was getting closer and closer to the other side. The two Paras had now stopped firing and were just staring at me as I slowly approached them. For a moment I thought, 'Is Lovat still behind or has he been hit?' I dared not look round. I was now across the bridge and level with the two Paras in the slit trench.

'I stopped playing the bagpipes and shook hands with the two Paras. Lovat, close behind me, was also safely across. A tall Airborne Officer approached us from across the road, his hand outstretched. Lieutenant 'Tod' Sweeney shook Lovat warmly by the hand and exclaimed, 'Very pleased to see you, old boy.'

'Lovat replied: 'And I am very pleased to see you, old boy. Sorry we are two and a half minutes' late!'

'The time was well after noon. I couldn't remember when I last ate something. The last main meal was yesterday in England. All of that came up on the bloody landing-craft on the way over. I was now feeling very hungry and thirsty.

'The commandos were streaming across the bridge and carrying three wounded with them. They laid the wounded at the side of the road. A corporal was telling a medic that there were a few casualties on the road leading from the Orne canal bridge.

'As we moved off I looked back at the Orne Bridge. The two Paras were still standing in their slit trench, looking a bit lonely I thought! Before the Brigade left England, at the last briefing we were told to expect the possibility that the Germans would have time to blow the bridges. Due to the good work done by the glider-borne troops in capturing both bridges intact, we were spared the problem of getting our feet wet again.

'There seemed to be a lot of firing going on in the vicinity of the canal bridge and to our right the sound of mortar explosions. We were now heading along a main road with wooded areas on both sides. We turned into a narrow, dusty lane with high hedgerows on either side. A short distance along the lane I saw up ahead a small group of cottages with some French people standing about looking at us as we approached. The adults were silent as we passed by, though the children seemed very interested in my bagpipes, but they kept well away from us, except a little girl aged about eight or nine years. She walked beside me for a short distance saying, 'Music, Music'... I blew up the bagpipes and played a tune for her, *The Nut Brown Maiden,* a very popular Scottish bagpipe tune. This drew a round of applause from the people in front of the cottages.

The little girl was very pretty, with long red hair over her shoulders. She was wearing a very old-looking white dress and her bare feet were in wooden clogs. As we continued our march along the lane I looked back and could see her still waving to us.

'I stop playing the bagpipes. We have been walking for about ten minutes and ahead I can see a crossroads. There is a lot of noise going on; mortars are exploding in the fields on the other side of the hedgerows. There appears to be a lot of activity and thick dust everywhere. The hedgerows are covered in dust and have a very odd appearance. On our left we pass the entrance to a quarry. As we reach the crossroads I observe on the other side a group of commandos coming down the road. They look tired; two of them are carrying a wounded comrade on a stretcher. It appears that an attack is being made on the village on the high ground at the top of the road. More wounded are coming from the road on my left. The mortar bursts are now very close and the scene at the crossroads looks very dangerous. The Germans up in the village have certainly got the range on our position. Lovat is standing in the centre of the crossroads and officers are approaching him from time to time and, judging by the expressions on their faces, things are not going too well. There is a large house on the left side of the crossroads; it has probably been a cafe or a restaurant.

'I entered the yard at the rear of the house and could see wounded being carried into a large barn on the far side of the yard. As I entered the barn and looked around I could see the place was almost full of wounded and dying commandos. They were all over the place, some lying down, others sitting up with their backs to the wall of the barn. They were being attended to by a couple of medics.

'I recognised several of the wounded, one in particular, Jim. He was lying on the straw-covered floor, badly wounded in the chest, his leg covered in blood. His face had a deathly pallor. I spoke to him, 'It's me Jim... Bill.' He just stared past me; his glazed eyes had no sign of recognition. Christ! It seemed just like a few hours ago when we were playing football together at the camp at Southampton. Three days ago, in fact.

'I felt a lump in my throat as I thought of his family in Newcastle. I had spent two days of my leave with them and his mum and dad had seen us off at the railway station on our way south to join the Brigade.

'I was beginning to wonder if there were many of us left. It seemed that soldiers were being killed and wounded since we had landed on the beach this morning. It's now late afternoon and it is still going on.

'I made my way back to the crossroads. Lovat is still there directing operations, oblivious to the mortars and the automatic fire. More wounded were being carried down the road to the quarry we had passed a short time ago. It was being used as a dressing station and as a fairly safe place to keep the wounded.

'I walked the short distance from the crossroads to the quarry. The wounded were being placed side by side at the far end. From time to time mortar bombs were bursting in the fields above the quarry, causing a certain amount of confusion among the wounded and those looking after them. It's only a matter of time until a mortar bomb lands in the quarry among the wounded. As I made my way back to the road there appeared to be a bit of excitement going on at the entrance to the quarry. As I drew closer I could see a vehicle with its nose in a ditch and two commandos were pulling someone from under it. An Officer was standing with his revolver drawn and shouting at the top of his voice, 'Get that bloody man out of there and back to the beach or I shall shoot him!' The two commandos pulled the soldier clear and hustled him down the road and away from the scene. The vehicle had been hit by a mortar blast and had gone off the road. The driver had either been hit by a mortar splinter or had gone round the twist at the sights around him. Whatever it was, he was a long way from the beach, that is, if the bridges over the Orne were still standing.

'As I left the quarry and made my way back up to the road to the crossroads, I noticed that more commandos were coming up from the Orne area. They were on either side of the road, sitting or standing in the ditches, waiting their turn to move up.

'Once again, I met my friends of No. 4 French Troop. They were sitting at the side of the road armed to the teeth with all kinds of weapons, British and German, bandoliers of ammunition criss-crossed over their chests. I had a few words with my friend Chauvet. He gave me three apples and a large bar of chocolate'.

Captain F. Vere Hodge MC RA, No. 1 Combined Operations Bombardment Unit:
'Our plane was caught in searchlights before we dropped and there was a good deal of tracer flying about. When my parachute opened I looked around; quite a lot was happening. I saw one parachute on fire and bullets started coming my way. I don't remember landing. I must have been knocked out for a few seconds because I found myself being dragged along the ground, the canopy still being filled with the stiff breeze. That was probably lucky for me; the chap firing at me probably thought he'd got me as I didn't get up. I caught the rigging lines, pulled them, collapsed the canopy, twisted the quick release box on my chest and threw off the harness. I had lost my helmet, surprisingly, as it was firmly strapped on with a chin piece as well as a strap. I put on my red beret. I found later that my dagger, strapped in its leather scabbard on my right leg, had pierced the leather and my trousers and made a small but annoying hole in my leg.

'There was no one near me but I sussed out where I thought I was and made towards what I hoped would be the prearranged rendezvous (RV) for my party along with part of 7 Para. I had a torch with a green light to identify myself as on 'our' side if necessary and as I got near the RV there were some green guiding lights. At the RV I found Alex and then Wilf Fortune arrived (dropping down into a fresh cowpat) and finally Ted Monks'.

Telegraphist Wilf Fortune: 'We all moved towards Bénouville, crossing Pegasus Bridge where we found 'A' Company in an orchard. When dawn broke, we found a house on the outskirts which would make a good Observation Post, tried the door. Locked. Round the back there were some steps down. Vere went down and this door was also locked, so he took his revolver out and shot the lock off. We burst in - the owner of the house was there with his two daughters. Vere explained in French that we were British but they would have none of it, saying, Allemands - 'Germans.' We went upstairs into the front bedroom from where we could see right across the fields. Alex got the radio out and we used a window on the landing. One of these ladies came up and took out the fur coats from the wardrobe, which made us laugh. Vere took his binoculars out for viewing the area. Then we saw the Germans coming very quickly towards 'A' Company. I said to Vere, 'They're on bikes Sir.' He said, 'No, they're running Wilfred.' I couldn't see their legs! Vere decided we had to warn the other lads so he told me and Ted to run and let them know. The attack happened shortly afterwards.'

Captain F. Vere Hodge: 'Alex continued trying to get a ship without success. There was a knock on the front door and the occupants spoke with a German soldier. Alex and I held our breath but they didn't give us away and the soldier left. The battle rolled past us and everything went quiet and I decided it was time to try and re-find the platoon who had been forced to withdraw. Calling on my French again I told the household, 'If I don't find my friends we will return here - 'ici.' They nodded but no one spoke. They were terrified, poor things. I've always been very appreciative of that family's courage; had the Germans caught them sheltering us they would have been shot on the spot. As Alex and I left the house everything was uncannily silent. There were one or two dead men lying in the road and one of our Airborne helmets lying by itself, which I put on and a German bandolier of ammunition, both of which I picked up. I then led the way over the road to a hedge and started to walk cautiously along it towards where I estimated 'A' Company might be, Alex following me. I hoped they would not shoot us. After some minutes of cautious progress I saw them and they saw me. They told us that Wilf had taken Ted on to find the First Aid Post.'

Will Fortune: 'One Sergeant was giving us a hard time because Ted was so slow in climbing a wall, so I said, 'Can't you see my mate's injured?' Be said to me, 'Sonny, we are the only ones left.' Ted was a big lad but that did not seem to matter lifting him up and over the wall. I took Ted to the First Aid post by the bridge and left him there. Ted was eventually taken home. By then I thought that Vere and Alex must have been captured, so I found another Forward Observation Unit under Captain Ritchie. I joined them and we went to do a shoot. Tosh Monks the Telegraphist was listening and he picked up a signal from Alex. I said, 'It looks like Captain Hodge is all right' and then the Captain said, 'What do you want to do?' I said, 'I think I should go back to them'.
'I crossed the bridge just as the seaborne troops crossed and the Paras pointed them out in a wood across this cornfield, but they warned me about snipers. I zigzagged across expecting a sniper's bullet at any time, but I made it and found Vere and Alex. Alex was signalling to the ships by Morse code to send the shells over. We had our position and the position of the enemy and we telegraphed that to the ship by Morse. Then the officer would give his 'Fall of Shot'. This was a reference to the target which is at the centre of the clock

face; the FOS is at six o'clock. Then 'Direction of Fall of Shot Landing'. A equals 100 yards, B equals 200 yards etc.

'Captain Hodge got a call that there were German 88-mm guns firing at the landing craft from Frenchville Plâge and we were sent to put it out of action. At first we wanted to use the top of a church tower - I remember that going up to the tower, we walked part of the way between the walls and a service was going on.

'Vere thought the lighthouse would be better so we used that. Alex was driving the jeep which we had the use of. A photographer rolled up, noticed Alec's Royal Navy badge and parachute wings and took a picture of the four of us in front of the lighthouse. The 88-mm guns were 800 yards away and we used letters for each 100 yards, so H was 800 yards and the direction was given as one o'clock, two o'clock etc. from our position. The ship had an artillery officer on board, but the ship also had to get itself in position for the shot so it might be ten minutes before anything happened. Then there would be the call from the ship, 'Fire for effect,' and the ranging shells would come over.

'A couple of days after we used the lighthouse the Germans shot the top off.' **For his part in this operation Wilf Fortune was Mentioned in Dispatches.**

About D-Day plus 2 I was asked to take my team into the grounds of Bénouville château where the fighting was a bit sticky. As we made our way there another COBU party met us coming back. The officer in charge, whom I knew slightly, told me that he had been up to the front but it was not possible to do a shoot.

'When we reached the château, the company commander told me that the Germans were pressing him from the other side of a large field, immediately outside the wooded château grounds. This target was technically too close to our own troops to engage because a ship's shell could fall on us. However, things didn't look too good anyway, so I decided to take the risk. The Tels got me a ship. I sent the fire orders and she fired but I couldn't see where the shots were falling. So I called for a battleship, thinking that as their shells weighed a ton or so if anything would show up on landing, they would. HQ attached me to a battleship codenamed PEG. The Tels told me afterwards that this was HMS *Ramillies*.

'I had a couple of ranging shots; they were just audible as they passed over our heads before landing, which caused some men near me to look askance, but I reassured them - the shells' landing was very visible. The next shots were right on target and the Germans came out of their bunker with a white flag. I sent the conventional code for 'shoot successfully completed' and added in plain language, 'Enemy considerably discouraged.'
Captain Vere Hodge. [14]

Bill Millin had just gone a few yards along the road when there was a loud swish and immediately an explosion on the other side of the hedgerow. 'As I landed in the ditch I could hear the mortar splinters crashing through the hedge and over my head. Someone cried out and suddenly everything was quiet. As

14 *Beachhead Assault: The Story of the Royal Naval Commandos in World War II* by David Lee (Greenhill Books and the Naval Institute Press, 2006)

I clambered out of the ditch there was a lot of dust hanging in the air. I seemed to be all right; at least I was not wounded. I examined the bagpipes and had a sinking feeling in my stomach when I noticed the large drone had been hit by the shrapnel and part of it had been shattered. Luckily the piece that was shattered could be repaired. Now I would have to rely on the two small drones. I placed the bagpipes in my rucksack and then continued to the crossroads. Lovat was still there and it appeared that Brigade HQ would not be entering the village today. There was still sporadic mortar and sniper fire as we moved a couple of hundred yards along the road to the right and occupied the farmhouse. The farmhouse was situated at the side of the road, with cornfields around it on three sides. Lovat entered the farmhouse as we all started to dig ourselves in. Some of the commandos were digging their slit trenches in and around the orchard, others at the edge of the cornfield, all the time we had to keep our heads down, due to the constant sniper fire coming from the area of the village on the high ground across the cornfields.

'I dug in at the edge of the road facing back the way we had come. I was joined by a corporal, a tall, beefy sort of chap, a Scotsman whom I had not met until today. Between us we dug a very good trench, big enough to hold both of us comfortably. The corporal went off and returned a few moments later with a PIAT gun and three bombs. I looked at the gun and the bombs that he was placing on the mound of earth at one end of the slit trench, the gun pointing along the road.

'Piper,' said the corporal, patting the PIAT gun. 'This is to knock out any fucking tanks that try to come along this road in front of us.' He squinted along the sights and continued, 'Let's hope the bastards don't get close enough for us to use it, right, Piper?' I nodded and thought that I had landed in France that morning armed only with a set of bagpipes, now I had a PIAT gun and three bombs. The corporal was busy in the trench so I went into the courtyard in front of the farmhouse. On the left, were the stables and hayloft and on the right, a chicken coop. The chickens had been removed and replaced by several German prisoners. Someone had been lucky with the chickens!

'I stood for a few moments looking through the wire of the chicken coop at the prisoners. These were more like the German soldiers we had been reading about in the newspapers and seeing on films. These prisoners were sullen, with a touch of arrogance about them. They were probably thinking that we commandos did not have much time left, before the German counter-attack drove us all back over the Orne and into the sea.

'The prisoners we had picked up west of the Orne were very poor specimens, probably eastern European types pressed into service with the German Army. This lot in the chicken coop were typical of the Germans facing us across the cornfields. They seemed determined to hold on to the high ground and the south of the village, also making their presence felt by their very accurate mortar and small arms fire. I entered the orchard at the side of the farmhouse, taking shelter from the constant sniping by keeping well down by a hedge.

'The orchard was surrounded on three sides by a low wall that had several holes blown into it by direct hits from the mortars. In the far corner, a British glider had nosedived into the orchard, its tail sticking high into the air and resting on the wall. The gliders had landed near the Orne bridges in the early hours, sometime after midnight, this one had probably gone off course. There was no sign of the occupants. Commandos were moving about the orchard, all of them crouching down to avoid the sniping. At the rear of the farmhouse I came across three commandos who had just finished digging a latrine. It was shaped like a slit trench and about two feet deep. There was a spar of wood across its length, resting on two large stones. In the British Army this was a duty that must be done, in action or out of action. The occupant of this latrine would sit on a spar, his arse facing the Germans across the cornfield, steadying himself by leaning on the wall of the farmhouse.

'Taffy, the latrine's first customer, had just dropped his trousers and had perched himself precariously on the spar, his very large and very white bottom in full view across the cornfields. The German snipers were very quick to respond to this horrible sight and several shots whistled over Taffy's head and thudded into the wall of the farmhouse, sending us all scattering for cover, including Taffy trying to run with his trousers round his ankles.

'The rifle shots were quickly followed by two mortar explosions near the orchard, setting off a barrage of oaths from a Sergeant who had to dive for cover to avoid the flying shrapnel. He surfaced a few seconds later to shout at Taffy, who was now trying to pull his trousers up.

'You bloody stupid Welsh bastard! If you want a shit, why don't you do what every other bastard's got to do? Go into the cornfield and keep your bloody head down!' This was the first laugh I had had since leaving England.

'When I arrived back at the gable end of the farmhouse 'Mac' the Corporal had made something to eat. The contents of a 24-hour ration pack taste quite good when one is hungry. He also produced two chicken legs and handed one to me. Best roast chicken I have ever tasted, bones and all. I decided not to ask him where he got the chicken legs. I had a suspicion that they had come from the chicken coop in the farmyard.

'We had been in the farm about two or three hours. Mac and I were sitting beside the slit trench chatting about the events of the day. He had just finished a couple of long bursts of Bren gun fire at the village and had settled down to clean the weapon. I had my bagpipes on the grass verge at the side of the road inspecting the damage done to them earlier on.

'There was the sound of a lot of activity coming from the farmyard. An officer appeared, ordering everyone out of the farm and to make their way across the road into the fields. Mac shouted to him, 'What's up, Sir?' 'Panzers corporal,' he exclaimed. The Panzers were heading this way from the direction of a village to the south, about three miles away. Mac picked up the PIAT gun and the Bren. I followed him across the road carrying his three PIAT bombs in their case, with the bagpipes under my left arm. We took up a position in line with the other commandos, lying face down behind a fairly large mound of turf that stretched away to the right, down a slope and towards the River Orne. We had crossed the Orne only a few hours ago and now the long-expected German counter-attack was on its way.

'As I lay behind the mound of earth staring straight ahead, I could not help thinking, 'How on earth are we going to stop the Panzers?' As far as I could see we had no anti-tank weapons, other than a few PIAT guns. Christ, what if we were forced to fall back to the Orne? I looked across the farm, where the wounded were being carried out and laid alongside the farmhouse wall. 'What a bloody time to be wounded,' I thought, as I watched the medics tending to their charges. I wondered what was passing through the minds of the wounded. If the Panzers over-ran our position they would have to be left behind.

'A commando was at the other end of the farmhouse with the German prisoners. He had them with their backs to the farmhouse wall and their hands above their heads. Earlier on they had looked sullen and arrogant, now they appeared terrified as they stared at the Bren gun the commando was pointing at them. He kept glancing round to see where we were, probably wondering what to do with the prisoners. To add to the confusion, the Germans up in the village seemed to be stepping up their mortaring of the farm area and this did not help any.

'We gazed out along the road waiting for the first sign of the Panzers. There were a few anxious faces in our group. Lovat came out of the farm and passed down the line of commandos. He glanced at the bagpipes on the grass beside me as he passed by.

'After about half-an-hour we were ordered back to the farm.

'It appeared that the Allied Air Force had broken up the Panzers' attack in our area.

'The sniper fire and the mortaring did not seem so bad now in the farm. At least we were still there and as long as we kept our heads down we stood a good chance of surviving.

'Evening was drawing in very quickly as Mac and I stood in our slit trench talking about something to eat. He went into his rucksack and brought out a dirty-looking little bundle of paper. He unwrapped the bundle and produced a chicken carcass. Tearing off a portion, he said, 'Get stuck into that, Piper. It may be your last!' We washed down the chicken and some of the 24-hour ration pack with a few mouthfuls of French cider that Mac had produced from his water bottle. I was thinking long may my friendship with Corporal Mac last; at least I wouldn't go short of something to eat.

'About 8.30 pm Mac and I were still in the slit trench looking out along the road towards the sea. We had a good view of the coast near to the mouth of the Orne. The evening and the scene in front of us could have easily been the South Coast of England, except, of course, for the sound of gunfire in the distance from the German batteries, who were now shelling the Orne bridges, possibly to try to prevent reinforcements reaching us. The shelling from the allied warships in the Channel had eased off. Their shells could be heard all day, passing overhead to fall with a loud explosion in the German positions. Even the local mortaring had gone quiet. There was still the odd sniper's bullet whistling through the trees in the orchard.

'Mac, don't you think it's getting a bit quiet?'

'The bastards are up to something,' was his quick reply, puffing on his cigarette. Then, just as quickly, he said, 'Piper, look at the sky over the coast! They are coming our way!' I looked towards the coast. I could see the dots above the horizon. They were in formation, so they must be aircraft. As the aircraft drew closer I could see that they were towing gliders. As the air armada got nearer and eventually passed over our positions, commandos were coming out from cover to gaze in fascination at the sight.

'The gliders were now being released from their tow-planes and were gliding, banking and turning over what seemed the whole area of Normandy. As Mac and I watched, one glider crashed into the cornfield, another smashed through the trees in the orchard. Others were being hit by enemy fire and I could see one glider crash into a row of houses on the outskirts of the village. Another made a perfect landing in the field across the road, slithering along the grass to a halt. The front dropped down and several Paras came tumbling out. They gathered their equipment and dashed across the fields.

'These airborne reinforcements were certainly a very welcome sight. As Mac and I watched the Paras landing all over the place, we suddenly felt very good and shook each other by the hand. There must be thousands of troops landing in this part of France. The anxious moments of earlier on gave way to a feeling of exultation and we all knew that the invasion, even at this early stage, was going to be successful. There was no way now that the German forces could push us back into the sea.

'Darkness had now come down and everything appeared peaceful. The mortaring from across the cornfields had ceased, except for the random sniper's bullet here and there. About a couple of miles away, near the coast; a lot of firing was going on.

'As I stood in the slit trench I could hear the German Artillery away in the distance still shelling the Orne area and the beaches. I could hear the bang of the guns and a short while later the moan of the shells high up as they passed over our positions, then the sound of explosions as the shells hit the ground.

'Before settling down for the night and taking our turn on watch, we decided to take a short walk and exercise our legs, along the short path at the side of the farmhouse. There was a strong smell of flowers and ripe corn in the air as we strolled along. The evening was peaceful and I felt very relaxed. We had gone only a few yards when suddenly there was a loud swish, followed immediately by two others and something exploded against the side of the farmhouse, high up. This was followed by two further explosions in the cornfield to the left.

'I threw myself to the ground and crawled swiftly in the direction of the slit trench. As I tumbled into the trench, my heart beating wildly, I could hear Mac's feet pounding along the path towards me. There was another explosion in the cornfield and the sound of flying shrapnel. Mac suddenly landed in the trench, almost on top of me, I moved over to make room for him as he gasped, 'I've been hit, Piper.'

'Where have you been hit?' He did not answer. I ran my hands over his chest and then his back. His back was sticky with blood and it was oozing all over his battledress. He did not answer when I spoke to him. I was sure he was dead. He was making no movement at all, just lying there on the floor of the trench. The explosions stopped as suddenly as they had begun and it was peaceful again.

'I crawled out of the trench and went into the farmyard looking for the medics. I found them in the barn with the wounded. One of the medics accompanied me back to the slit trench to have a look at Mac. We lifted him out of the trench and carried him into the barn. The medic gave him a quick examination and said, 'He is dead.' He had several pieces of shrapnel in his back and in the back of his head there was also a wound. As I left the barn they were pulling a blanket over Mac's head.

'I returned to the trench at the side of the road and a few moments later a commando joined me to help man the PIAT gun. 'You get the head down, Piper... I'll do the first watch.'

'As I huddled at the bottom of the trench alone with my thoughts, it seemed a long time since we had boarded the craft on the Hamble River. The smiles and the cheers as we sailed past all the ships waiting their turn to sail to France; the sea journey, the sickness, the desperation to get off the heaving landing-craft. Landing on the beaches, the march to the Orne and now, sitting here in a slit trench at the edge of a cornfield in France.

'A lot had happened in fourteen hours. It had all been like a dream, the events of the day all running into each other, with no time to think or to assess what was going on, or to even think of the dangers. The pallor of the faces of the wounded, first seen on the beach, had remained strongly on my mind. It was strange to think that a friend who was alive such a short time ago, drinking a pint of beer in an English pub, was now lying in a ditch at the side of the road, with a piece of shrapnel in his head.

'The end of the first day of the invasion and this far, I had been very lucky'.

'Evening now and the sky suddenly filled with a vast number of gliders and aircraft dropping supplies in the bridge area. A most welcome sight. We knew now that we had more tanks and mobile guns and more comrades with us. A plane was hit by German anti-aircraft guns and came down in flames crashing in a nearby field. For us sappers by the Canal Bridge it now meant an all night guard duty. Certainly a very long and eventful day.

'On D+2 a FW 190 fighter-bomber flew in very low over the River Bridge and then dropped a bomb on the Canal Bridge. I watched, as the bomb was released, about 200 yards from its target. I said to myself, 'You've had it!' I was about ten yards from where the bomb fell but it did not explode. A lump of rag placed in the mechanism had sabotaged (the bomb!) If it had exploded I would not have survived. We hit the deck at great speed. I was hit by a piece of shrapnel. Claude was hit at the same time but suffered less injuries. I was stretchered on to a French Resistance lorry and taken almost instantly to a beach First Aid Station. In due course I was told I was to be taken back to the UK. Inside this huge Tank Landing Craft many stretcher cases arrived. I was one of the first batches delivered. I wasn't sure what had happened to Claude. I asked an attendant if someone like me, as he was my twin brother, had arrived. 'Yes,' he replied, 'he was in the last load aboard.'

'Hospitalised together for a couple of weeks with plenty of humour and care from the nurses and then I was moved on alone for a further two months to another hospital and we both rejoined 249 Company in September.'

Sapper Cyril Larkin.

'I stayed in France from 6 June to 6 September and it was horrific... there were so many casualties. I was very lucky. Normandy was a killing ground… likened to Stalingrad in terms of loss of German and Allied lives. The pallor of the faces of the wounded remained strongly in my mind. There was no time to feel real emotion. 'People on opposing sides were so close that you could hear them speaking and after a while, you could even distinguish who was about to fire by the sound of the bomb going down the barrel of the mortar. Jock, my friend of many years ago, had taken me off to find some shelter in a dugout, giving at least some protection from the flying shrapnel. German mortars were exploding. Two explosions in quick succession made me throw myself to the ground. They seemed so close, right behind me... I lay on the ground for a few moments; there were no further explosions. As I warily got to me feet I felt a compulsion to retrace my steps in the direction of Jock's trench. He lay on the grass, a large open wound at the back of his head and one of his legs was missing. His green beret lay close by. A piece of shrapnel had hit his cap badge and had penetrated the front of his skull. The cap badge with its St. Andrews Cross split in two brought a lump to my throat as I stood rooted to the spot. Stretcher-bearers were quickly on the scene, taking two wounded commandos away and leaving Jock lying on the grass. There was nothing they could do for him. No doubt they would return and place him with the other commando dead in neat rows in front of the château to await burial.

'When the campaign was over instead of going to visit my parents in Glasgow, I went straight back to Fort William to see a woman I had met during my training. I was very much in love with her. Girls had been very thin on the ground - they were generally regarded as an unnecessary distraction. When our friendship had developed I would stay at the cottage. We tried to keep it a secret but that had proved impossible. When I got back I discovered that she had died in hospital while I had been in Normandy. It was probably cancer, but no one asked about such things then. I stayed at her cottage for a few days afterwards, going out onto the hills and playing my pipes. It was my way of coming to terms with my emotions.

'I think she had known she was going to die all along. She seemed to have a kind of sixth sense about the future. A few weeks before I was given the orders to leave Scotland, she had told me that Lord Lovat was going to take me away from her. I didn't believe her at that stage, but it was all true. She also told me that Lord Lovat would be injured within seven days of the fighting, which he was. On 12 June he was hit in his back by a lump of shrapnel during an attack.

'I doubt if any pipers will play in action again. But then I doubt there will ever be another Lord Lovat.'

Piper Bill Millin. Simon 'Shimi' Fraser, 17th Baron Lovat, 25th chief of the Clan Fraser, was repatriated to England after being severely wounded during 6 Commando's battle for Bréville Wood on 12 June. (His friends called him 'Shimi', an anglicised version of his name in the Scottish Gaelic language). He became under Secretary of State for foreign affairs in 1945.

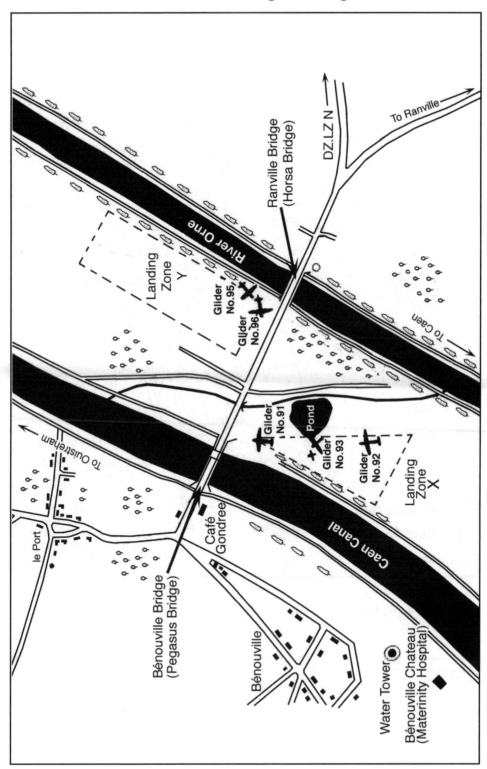

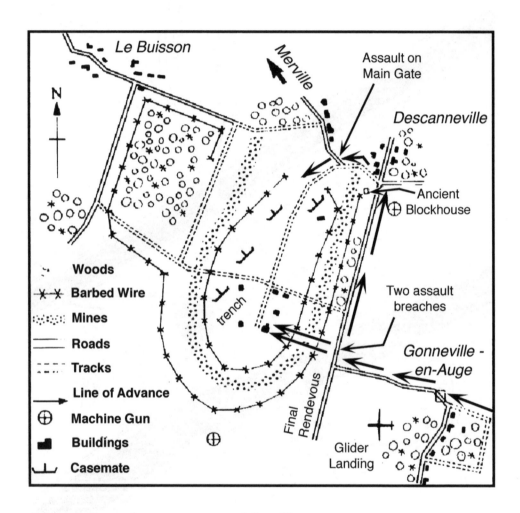

The attack on the casemates at Merville.

Chapter 3

Merville - The Red Devils' Greatest Triumph

*'Terence Otway was 29 and looked younger; and at that age he commanded 750
of the toughest of British troops. He was slim and lightly built. His face was lean
and gave an impression of keen intellect and an ascetic and sensitive character.
One might almost have been forgiven for putting him down, at first sight, as an
artist rather than a colonel of paratroops. But such appointments are more than a
matter of chance. Otway's father had been killed in the First World War and his
mother had had a long struggle to bring up her son on a war widow's pension.
When he left school he was nearly articled to a solicitor in Brighton; but he hated
the idea of settling down in an office before he had seen the world at all and so,
when he was 19 he had entered the Royal Military College, Sandhurst and been
commissioned into the army, only intending to stay for five years. The army took
him to the north-west frontier of India and to China. The five years expired a few
months before war began. By then, he had come to despise a good many things
about army life, especially life in an officers' mess in India and he had tried to get
out. But he had not been allowed to go; and so, by D-Day, he had served for ten
years and had revealed-perhaps to his own surprise - an extremely acute and
incisive military brain.'*
Dawn of D-Day by David Howarth.

'When I was given the task of capturing Merville Battery early in 1944 I
realised that it was going to be a very a complicated operation and a very
tough one. We would be jumping over the Atlantic wall in order to land on
another fortress. And we were going to drop and move up to attack at night.
So I determined that every single man from the most senior officer down to
the youngest and junior private must know exactly what he and everyone
else was doing. With the use of air photographs and models I decided to
construct a replica of the battery as similar as possible to what we could see
in the air photos and the staff found a place at Inkpen in Berkshire where
there is an 800 feet cliff so that we could use live ammunition. With the help
of the Royal Engineers, we constructed the approach as near as possible; that
is to say if there was a ditch on the photo and it wasn't in Berkshire, we made
a ditch. If there was a stile we made a stile. We rehearsed the operation nine
times and then when we went into the transit camp where we were sealed
for ten days we went through the whole thing again using models.

'I was concerned about security. Obviously, if there was any breach it would have been a disaster. I asked if I could have twelve WAAFs in civilian clothes - glamorous, attractive, beautiful girls and I gave the battalion 24 hours leave in Newbury and sent these girls there. I told them before they went that they could use any means at their disposal to try and get the troops to tell them something about what was going on. And I left the 'any means' to their discretion. The result was whatever means they used or did not use, they didn't get any single thing out of the troops. I never enquired what 'means' they used. [15]

Lieutenant Colonel Terence Otway, CO, 9th Battalion, Parachute Regiment.

'Of the [3rd Parachute Brigade's] tasks, none was more important than that of destroying the battery at Map Reference 15576 near the little village of Merville. The battery in question consisted, it was thought, of four 150 mm guns established in concrete emplacements twelve feet high and five feet deep, the thickness of the concrete walls being six feet six inches and the roof above them covered with thirteen feet of earth. All doors which gave access to the position were made of steel and the main armament was defended by one twenty mm dual-purpose gun which could be used to combat attack from the air or land and several machine-guns - the exact number was uncertain. The position was surrounded by a cattle fence which enclosed a minefield 100 yards in depth. This was bordered on its inner side by a barbed wire fence fifteen feet thick and five feet high and in many places this fence had been doubled. At the seaward side of the battery was an anti-tank ditch fifteen feet wide and ten feet deep. To complete the defences, additional minefields had been laid across all the open approaches to the battery and machine-guns had been sighted to cover them. It will be generally agreed that these defences were in the last degree formidable. They were held by between 180 and 200 men.

'This, then, was the nut which had to be cracked and the nutcrackers consisted of the 9th Battalion of the Parachute Regiment and three gliders manned by volunteers, whose stern duty it would be to land not near but on the battery. This was only possible if the pilots were prepared to crash-land their gliders and to rely on the concrete defences of the battery to tear off their wings, thus arresting the progress of the fuselages, which would contain three officers and forty-seven other ranks of the Battalion and one officer and seven other ranks of the Royal Engineers.

To Lieutenant-Colonel T. B. H. Otway of the Royal Ulster Rifles was entrusted the formidable duty of silencing this battery and he took over his

15 The maintenance of secrecy was of vital importance. To secure it, all roads leading to the area were closed and no one without a pass signed by the Commanding Officer himself could make use of them. Most of the local landed gentry accepted these restrictions cheerfully, but a number, eager to maintain the rights of property, had to be pacified by drinks in the Mess. To make sure that every officer and man was maintaining his pledge of secrecy a number of specially trained and attractive young women were sent into the area with orders to do their utmost to extract information from the troops. Their failure was complete. Nothing was revealed, although the whole plan had been deliberately divulged by Brigadier Hill to every officer and man, the only information withheld being the actual time and place of the attack. *By Air To Battle: The Official Account of the British Airborne Divisions.*

command on April 2nd. His planning and preparations provide the promised example of how meticulously the preliminary measures are carried out before an airborne assault is delivered. After considering the problem for a week, he asked for and was given carte blanche in the matter of the rehearsals and other preparations indispensable for success. He chose a spot in England near Newbury, where conditions very similar to those which, would be met with in Normandy prevailed. The land was under cultivation and the crops on it valued at several thousand pounds; but the necessities of war were paramount. Otway asked for the use of it on a Wednesday and the Sappers began work upon it on the following Friday, permission to do so having been obtained in the meantime from seven different Ministries in Whitehall. A complete and accurate reproduction of the battery 400 yards by 400 yards was constructed in a week, its shape and dimensions being determined from the numerous air photographs available. Tubular scaffolding was used to simulate the guns. In order to reproduce the exact conditions it was necessary not only to build the model to scale but also to level the ground covering the approaches to it. Four mechanical excavators and six large bulldozers, brought to the area by tank transporters from cities as far away as Liverpool and Plymouth, worked night and day, the hours of darkness being illumined by headlights. Thirty-five officers and 600 other ranks were continuously practised over a number of weeks till everyone knew his own precise duty and how to carry it out. Five rehearsals by day and four by night, all conducted with live ammunition, sufficed to give the troops an exact idea of what it was they were to accomplish.

'On 31 May, after the battalion had moved from this training area to the

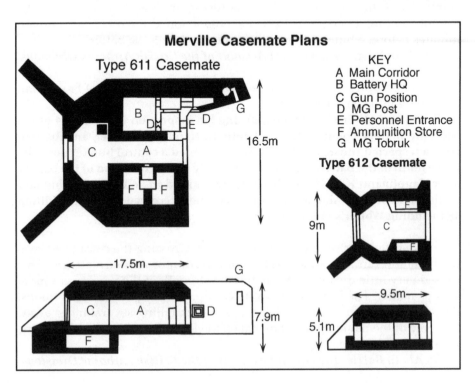

Merville Casemate Plans

Type 611 Casemate

KEY
A Main Corridor
B Battery HQ
C Gun Position
D MG Post
E Personnel Entrance
F Ammunition Store
G MG Tobruk

Type 612 Casemate

airfields from which they would take off, the special briefing for the operation was begun. It lasted five days and every man attending it was required to submit to his immediate superior his own sketch, drawn from memory, of the part he had to play. The troops to be carried in the gliders had been chosen from volunteers called for from the battalion - no easy task, for not one man but demanded to be set in the post of utmost danger. Let it be remarked in passing that not only would the gliders have to crash-land on the battery; but they would have to do so under heavy fire from the assaulting Parachute Battalion. On the morning of June 5th a drumhead service was conducted by the Reverend Gwinett, at which a special flag made by the Women's Voluntary Service of Oxford was dedicated and before the take-off that evening, the Commanding Officer spoke personally to every officer and man in the battalion.

'The plan provided for two special parties to be dropped in advance, one to organize the rendezvous, the other to reconnoitre the battery. A third under the Second-in-Command was to create a firm base, while other parties were detailed to snipe the defenders of the battery and to create a diversion against any German troops in the immediate neighbourhood. The main body of the battalion was to form the breaching and assault formations. They were to be provided with special equipment, carried in five gliders and including anti-tank guns, jeeps loaded with ammunition and scaling ladders with which to cross the anti-tank ditch. Three gaps were to be blown in the battery defences by demolition parties and the rest of the battalion would then enter the battery and there join their glider borne comrades in the task of killing or capturing anyone they found. As the assault went in, a party was to create a diversion at the main gate and ten minutes before, a hundred Lancasters were to bomb the battery.

By Air To Battle: The Official Account of the British Airborne Divisions.

'Whoever occupies this field will hold the key to the gateway of France and eventually into Germany itself.'

Feldmarschall Erwin Rommel, during his inspection in June 1944 of the Merville Battery commanded by Leutnant Raimund Steiner, an Austrian from a respected Innsbruck family, who occupied a control bunker one mile to the north of the Battery. Steiner had recently taken command of the battery after Hauptmann Karl-Heinrich Wolter was killed in an RAF bombing raid on the night of 19/20 May when the officers' mess received a direct hit, killing 18 including Wolter's French girl friend.

'The take-off gave rise to no special incident. Crossing the coast of France, the battalion ran into a moderate concentration of anti-aircraft fire. This caused very little disorganization, but the strength of the wind was a more serious matter. The Dakotas of No. 46 Group, carrying the airborne troops, dropped them over a very wide area; one stick falling several miles away, for some of the navigators had mistaken the River Dives for the River Orne which was the pin-point.'

By Air To Battle: The Official Account of the British Airborne Divisions

'I actually stood in the door of my aircraft when we flew over the Solent and it was a most fantastic sight. It was bright enough to see quite a lot of detail. I could see all the ships in the Solent. They seemed to be in a ring round the Isle of Wight and they seemed to be already streaming towards the French coast. Our plan was to drop on the dropping zone side and to attack at 04:30 and have three glider-loads of troops land inside the battery, stopping themselves by knocking their wings off the casements and taking the garrison entirely by surprise. The last part of the gliders' journey would be lit up by mortar flares laid by us.

'I'd planned four attack parties for the casements, one for each casement and therefore four gaps in the wire to be blown up by what were called Bangalore torpedoes. And I had two diversion parties: one to go to the main gate and kick up a hell of a row and one to go to the left and kick up a hell of a row, to divert the garrison. There was an anti-tank ditch on the seaward side of the battery, I presume they expected tanks to come in across the beach there and I wasn't sure whether that ditch would be extended round to our side so I'd had special lightweight bridges made. I also took with me, in gliders, some anti-tank guns to blow down the rear steel doors of the casements should they be shut: there was no point in attacking the battery and trying to get through a steel door. I also took Royal Engineers to blow the guns up and I took Royal Navy telegraphers because I was told that if we had not succeeded by 05:50 HMS *Arethusa* would bombard the battery and these men, who dropped with us, were to direct the fire. So that, in outline, was the plan.'

Lieutenant Colonel Terence Otway, CO, 9th Battalion, Parachute Regiment.

'Anti-aircraft fire began as they crossed the coast of France; and not many seconds later, Otway had his first warning that the drop was going to go wrong. The pilot began to throw the aircraft about in violent evasive action. The effect on the drill of the parachutists was chaotic. When they tried to move down to the door to jump in the quick compact succession for which they were trained, the sudden lurches threw them off their balance. Some fell on the floor encumbered by their heavy equipment. Others tripped over them in struggling cursing heaps. Out of the melee, Otway shouted to the pilot: 'Hold your course, you bloody fool.'

'We've been hit in the tail,' one of the aircrew shouted back.

'You can still fly straight, can't you?' Otway asked angrily. But before he was given an answer, the signal came to jump. Otway's turn was early. He clambered along to the door and found he was still clutching the half-empty bottle of whisky. [16]

He thrust it at the RAF dispatcher. 'You're going to need this,' he said; and with that parting shot, he jumped.

16 For the 24 hours before the attack, Otway had put a ban on alcohol, in case anyone under the strain of waiting drank too much and went into battle with a hangover. But he had broken his own rule to the extent of taking a bottle of whisky with him and somewhere over the Channel he woke up and passed it round the twenty men in his aircraft. They did not drink much, or perhaps they had quietly thought of providing themselves with something. The bottle came back to him before it was empty.

'...Below him were fields with thick black hedges and across the fields, downwind, a farmhouse which he knew particularly well. It was the last place he wanted to land; for it was ringed with blue on his map and marked as a German battalion headquarters. Otway was still angry at the way his men's training had been nullified by the pilot's tactics. He was made angrier by finding now that the aircraft had been off course and angrier still by seeing that somebody was shooting at him. Tracers were passing him; looking up, he saw them tearing through his parachute. It struck him as damned impertinence, but there was not much time to worry about it because the wind was drifting him straight to the German headquarters. He tried to manipulate his parachute to keep clear of the place, but there was nothing much he could do. Inexorably, as he fell, the wind took him, at 15 mph, across the last field and then across the farmyard. He hit the wall of the house itself, some feet above the ground and dropped out of his harness into what seemed to be a garden. Two of his men were there already. A German threw open an upstairs window and leaned out. One of the men with Otway picked up a brick and threw it. It was a good shot. There was a crash of glass and the German put his head in and Otway and his companions ran by instinct to the back of the house and got out of the garden while the German headquarters staff poured out of the front door.

'Otway learned later that only seven of the twenty men in his plane had managed to disentangle themselves in time to jump while it was over the dropping zone. It had to make three more runs to get them all out. Among the seven who jumped with him was Wilson his batman [who] had been a professional boxer and a professional valet and nobody could have had better qualifications as an airborne colonel's batman; but his drop was even unluckier than his colonel's... The German headquarters building had a greenhouse attached to it and Wilson went plumb through the roof and landed in a shower of broken glass among the pot plants. At that moment, the Germans were rushing out of the building and he rushed out behind them and found himself being shot at by some Canadians. None the worse, he set off for the rendezvous alone.'

Dawn Of D-Day **by David Howarth.**

'By ten minutes to three in the morning only 150 out of 600 men had reached the rendezvous and were ready to begin the approach march to the objective. One of them was the Commanding Officer, who, with the rest of his stick, had been flung untimely out of his Dakota as it was taking evasive action to avoid the flak. Lieutenant-Colonel Otway found himself heading straight for the roof of what he knew to be the headquarters of a German battalion. So accurately and clearly had the maps and models been prepared that, though he had never been there before, he knew exactly where he was. Missing the headquarters house by a few feet, he landed in the garden with one other man, who picked up a brick and flung it through a window through which the Germans were firing at them with revolvers. Presumably mistaking it for a bomb the enemy fled. Otway then made his way to the rendezvous, leaving behind him, unknown to himself, Wilson, his batman, who had fallen through the roof of the greenhouse, but who subsequently rejoined him.

By Air To Battle: The Official Account of the British Airborne Divisions

'I arrived at the rendezvous about one o'clock, maybe earlier, to be met by Wilson my batman - and here I am not exaggerating - who said, 'Shall we have our brandy now, sir?' He was an ex-valet and he literally held out to me a flask of brandy he had taken - my flask of whisky had been smashed on landing. I then found that out of the total group strength of around 750, that's to say the 650-odd of the battalion plus the artillerymen for the anti-tank guns, the medical men who dropped with us, the sailors, the engineers, I only had a hundred of all ranks, including myself.

'Unbeknown to everybody else I'd kept a quarter of an hour on the timing up my sleeve as a cushion and in that time another fifty came in. But I was then faced with the decision: 'I'm supposed to attack this battery with a battalion of six hundred-odd men, excluding the ones coming in on the gliders and I've only got 150.' I had no wireless sets. I had one machine gun and I had ten Bangalore torpedoes out of forty to blow the gaps with. I had no bridges in case we had to cross the anti-tank ditches. So far as I was aware, I had no anti-tank guns, no sailors, one doctor and very few medical people. So the question was, do I go on with 150? Or do I pack it in? 'I don't know what I'm going to do, Wilson' I said. He replied, 'There's only thing, sir.' And that was it. That gave me the incentive to carry on.

'So we moved off at 02:15, following the path which we knew so well so from photographs. We heard a German anti-aircraft battery firing, I suppose, not more than a hundred yards from us on our left and some of the soldiers wanted to go for that and I wouldn't let anybody do that, that wasn't our job and we let them get on with it.

'A farm halfway to the battery was the rendezvous to where Major Smith was due to come back from his job with the reconnaissance party, which he did. He told me that they had had no mine detectors and no tape for marking paths through the minefield. But he also said Paul Greenway and another man had cut the wires, had crawled through the minefield, neutralising the mines with their fingers and had then sat on their backs sides and dragged their heels on the ground, making a path through the minefield. Quite extraordinary. But I was faced now with two gaps instead of four to put in four parties against the encasements and I had to completely re-plan. I simply cut my encasement assault parties right down to the maximum one could get out of 150 soldiers and would put in two parties through each gap.

'We then moved on towards the battery and we found that the RAF had mostly missed it. There were a hundred Lancasters in support of my operation, each carrying a thousand-pound bomb and they had missed the battery but they had successfully bombed our route without knowing it, so we had to go in and out of these huge craters. And when we were about halfway between the farmhouse and the battery we heard a noise of troops moving and we guessed it was a German patrol. They didn't seem to be making any effort to conceal themselves and we all lay down and they passed so close to us we could have reached out and caught them by the ankles, but they didn't see us or hear us.

'And we moved on.'

Lieutenant Colonel Terence Otway, CO, 9th Battalion, Parachute Regiment.

'A chap was brought in with the top of his head blown off, brains spilling out into the stretcher. The Medical Orderly (MO) took one look at him. I said, 'Is there anything we can do?' He shrugged. So I gave him a lethal shot of morphine. When the MO came back, I told him. He said, 'It's OK, you did quite right. If he'd lived, he'd have been a vegetable for the rest of his days.' I am sure there were others like this. But we did not talk about it.'

Private James Bramwell, 9th Parachute Battalion, 6th Airborne Division.

'I am afraid we all felt a bit gloomy about the prospects - strong winds and lumpy seas! Changing visibility and it seemed a desperate venture to try to make a landing on a defended coast under such conditions. However the decision was taken and early on Monday morning, June 5, I was able to broadcast to my ship's company. The die is cast, we are committed to the attack and now it must be driven home at all costs - here is the general plan and the part we are called upon to play. About 3.15 we had a brief lull, which enabled me to get a much needed cup of coffee from my thermos and a sandwich, but we were soon at work again on our particular battery. The trouble was that he was a new one with concrete casemates for his guns and only direct hits would do permanent harm. We settled down to a prolonged strafe and got many shells firmly into the battery area and we knew that we secured hits on at least two of the casemates. Early in the afternoon a follow-up wave went ashore and the RAF put a smashing bomb attack on top of our battery which added to our efforts.'

Admiral Middleton, captain of HMS *Ramillies*.

'Once arrived at the rendezvous, Otway found the state of affairs far less favourable than he had hoped. To quote from his staccato official report: 'By 0250 hours the battalion had grown to 150 strong with twenty lengths of Bangalore torpedo. Each company was approximately thirty strong. Enough signals to carry on - no three-inch mortars - one machine-gun - one half of one sniping party - no six-pounder guns - no jeeps or trailers or any glider stores - no sappers - no field ambulance, but six unit medical orderlies - no mine detectors - one company commander missing. The Commanding Officer decided to advance immediately.'

'The hearts of the more fortunate remained unshaken, even when, on moving forward, they were attacked by a herd of maddened cows rushing wildly across a field in the quiet moonlight. Fortunately the reconnaissance party had been dropped in the right place. They had been somewhat shaken by the bombing attack of the Lancasters, for it 'had missed the battery completely' but the bombs had fallen very close to the reconnaissance party. By the time the advance began, this party had cut gaps in the outer cattle fence, penetrated the minefield and lain down for half an hour beside the inner belt of wire, where they observed the enemy posts; discovering their exact whereabouts by listening to the conversation of the sentries. They were presently joined by a party whose duty it was to lay white tapes to show the way. Only half of these men had been delivered at the right place and all the tapes were missing. The approaches were therefore marked 'by digging heel marks in the dust.' This vital preliminary work was accomplished without the loss of a single man, though those engaged on it were without mine detectors and had to neutralize the various trip wires by feeling for them with their hands.

'Meanwhile the much-depleted battalion, heavily shelled by guns firing on fixed lines, was advancing to the assault. On reaching the position chosen for the firm base, they came under the fire of six enemy machine-guns. The battalion's solitary machine-gunner was sent to do his best to quieten these. He silenced the fire of three of them. The other three were put out of action by the party moving against the main gate. As the battalion reached the outer defences two of the three gliders - the tow rope of the third had parted early and it had landed in England to the chagrin of its occupants - appeared circling overhead. It had been decided to signal to them by firing flares from the mortars; but there were no mortars, no flares and consequently no signals.

'The pilot of the leading glider, Staff Sergeant S. G. Bone had had to overcome many difficulties on the way over. Weather conditions were unfavourable, with much cloud, which had to be avoided as far as possible by weaving. In mid-Channel the arrester parachute gear, a device designed to check the speed of a glider as it comes in to land, opened suddenly. This mishap caused the combination to stall and lose height. The gear was jettisoned immediately, but the tail unit of the Horsa had been badly strained. On reaching the French coast, flying beneath cloud which was 10/10ths at 1,000 feet, the combination came under anti-aircraft fire and was repeatedly hit. Nevertheless, the Albemarle tug, with Pilot Officer Garnett at the controls, flew steadily on and circled what was believed to be the objective four times before releasing the glider. On the way down, Staff Sergeant Bone at first thought that the village of Merville was the battery, but at 500 feet he realized his mistake, turned away and landed eventually about half a mile from the objective.

'The other glider, piloted by Staff Sergeant D. F. Kerr had four casualties from flak when crossing the coast and, like its predecessor, was towed four times round the area before release. Coming in to land, Kerr saw that he would not quite be able to reach the battery. He therefore streamed his parachutes and crashed into an orchard only fifty yards from the perimeter. Though he had failed to put his passengers into the very midst of the enemy in accordance with the plan, yet they were able to play a very important part in the fight; for hardly had they left the glider when they encountered a German platoon hurrying to reinforce the garrison of the battery.

Outnumbered more than two to one and dazed by the shock of their landing, the troops and the glider pilots nevertheless defended the orchard with the greatest vigour for four hours. Not a single man of the enemy got through to help the hard-pressed defenders of the battery.

'Hard-pressed indeed, for Otway was pushing his assault regardless of the consequences. Two gaps were blown by the Bangalore torpedoes in the wire; then the attackers streamed in and at once engaged in hand to hand fighting with the German gunners. These offered a stout resistance until one of them, seeing the badges of his opposite, screamed Paratruppen whereupon such as were left alive, twenty-two in number, surrendered. The guns, which were found to be seventy-five mm, were then destroyed by gammon bombs.

'So at a cost of five officers and sixty-five other ranks killed or wounded, was accomplished a fine feat of arms whose success was of the greatest help to the seaborne invading forces. Among the victors was the battalion signals officer, who was seen by his Colonel to be fumbling in the blouse of his battledress. 'What are you doing?' asked Otway. 'Sending a signal home, sir,' was the answer and from his breast he withdrew a somewhat crumpled carrier pigeon, which arrived in England a few hours later with a message recording the success of the operation.'

By Air To Battle: The Official Account of the British Airborne Divisions.

'I got along to the RV and saw Colonel Otway looking very peculiar indeed. The reason was that there was hardly anybody there. I was the junior subaltern of 'C' Company and when he saw me he said, 'You're commanding 'C' Company. Well, don't stand there. Get on, go and see your company.' My company was about five men. Gradually it dawned on us that something had gone frantically wrong. The plan that Colonel Otway had devised for this operation was exceedingly complex, so complex that it was like a multiple chain that depended on each individual link and the links were all disappearing one by one before our eyes, at this stage.

'I had to go back and report to him every quarter of an hour how many men there were. Two of my men were in a dreadful state, one had lost his rifle and the other had lost his helmet and his rifle and we'd been told - it was more of a threat than an intention - that any man losing his rifle would be court-martialled. A silly threat, because you can't have court-martials in battle, but it was sufficient to upset these two chaps very much. So I tried to cheer them up by saying that we'd soon be able to find some German rifles for them and it would be all right. Then, at last, Lieutenant Parfitt arrived. He was just senior to me and I very proudly said, 'Here's your company. You can take it over now, you're senior to me' and he goggled. We'd got about ten men by then, I suppose. It was really lamentable.

'Colonel Otway waited as long as he dared before moving off. Greenway and his mine-lifting party had already gone on but with no mine detectors and no tape. They were meant to have arrived in gliders on our dropping zone immediately after we'd come down but there had been no gliders there. Three-inch mortars hadn't arrived either and one three-inch mortar

Avro Lancaster LM446 on 619 Squadron which was one of five Lancasters lost on the raid on Gennevilliers on 9/10 May during the pre-invasion build up. At Pointe-du-Hoc the gun positions, which were considered to be the most dangerous battery of all, were bombed throughout May, with a heavier than average attack by both day and night three days before D-Day and it received the heaviest and most concentrated attack of the night of 5/6 June with 637 tons being dropped on it by 108 Lancasters of 5 Group.

Handley Page Halifax III of RAF Bomber Command. On 5/6 June Halifaxes and Stirlings on 138, 149 and 161 Squadrons dropped dummy parachutists, rifle fire simulators and other devices such as squibs and fireworks, which produced the sound of gunfire to help confuse the German defenders on D-Day.

Boeing B-17 Flying Fortresses dropped 500-pound bombs leaving this crater-marked beach area at Arromanches, France on the Normandy invasion coast. Coastal gun sites and an observation posts, all under construction as well as the beach ahead were also bombed.

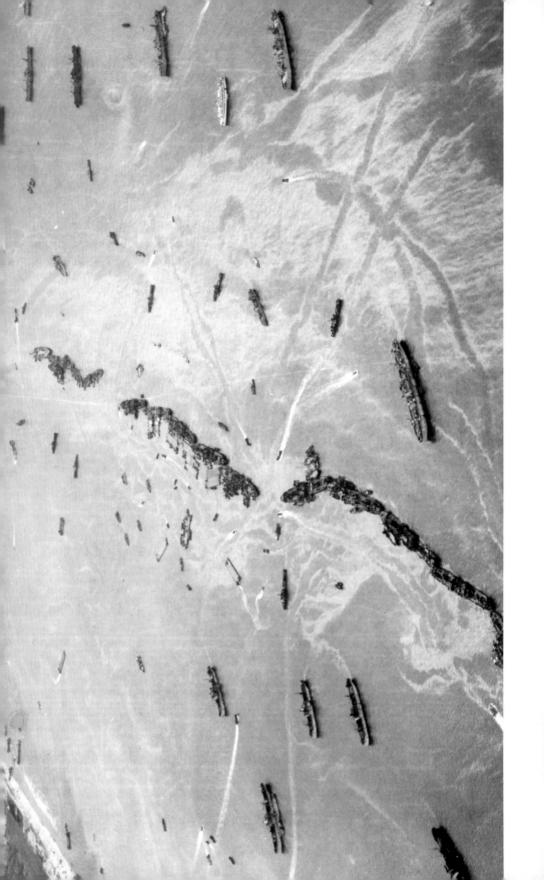

British Glider pilots decorated at Buckingham Palace, 1944: Staff Sergeants Bruce Hobbs, Stan Pearson, Wally Herbert, Jim Wallwork (all DFMs) and Tommy Moore, MM.

Preceeding page: American Liberty ships were deliberately scuttled off the beaches to provide makeshift breakwaters during the early days of the invasion somewhere in France. This scene shows 13 Liberty ships formed into a protecting screen for the vessels unloading on Omaha beach.

Eight men were killed when their Horsa glider was destroyed landing near Hiesville .

Two views of Pointe de Hoc from the air.

Above: A low-level reconnaissance picture taken just before the invasion.

Below: Pointe du Hoc undergoes attack from A-20 medium bombers of the Ninth Air Force striking on June 4, 1944, the beginning of two days of intense bombardment and naval shelling leading up to the assault on D-Day.

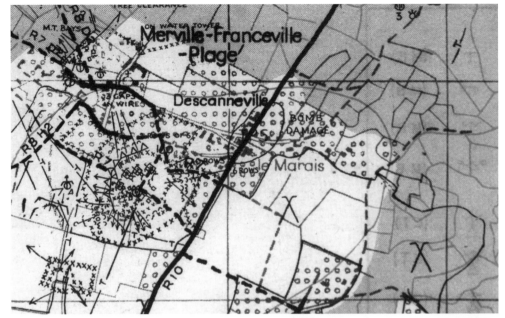

Map of Merville Franceville Plage.

Right: Leutnant Raimund Steiner, an Austrian from a respected Innsbruck family, who occupied a control bunker one mile to the north of the Merville Battery on D-Day.

Left: 19-year old Emil Courteil and his Alsatian paratroop dog 'Glen' of the 9th Parachute Battalion who were killed trying to make their way back to the Merville battery when they were strafed by RAF aircraft. Both are buried in Ranville War Cemetery.

WK

WK

GSGS 4347 40/16 NE
155776

GARDEN WIRE

N

13 METRES

100   0   100   2

SCALE   IN   YARDS

MERVILLE   Medium Troop   Interservice Target No. 10/J/81

Ref Map: GSGS 4250/7F2/155776. Chart Map F.1016.
Geographical Coordinates: 49° 16' 15" N. 00° 11' 52" W.
Height above sea level: 13 meters.

Four 150mm (5.9 in) howitzers. Range 14,600 yards. Weight of shell 96 lbs.
Rate of fire 5 r.p.m. Guns in casemates 56 – 66 yards apart. Number 1 casemate
is 59 feet by 52 feet and includes compartments for personnel and ammunition.
Thickness of concrete about 6½ feet. The sides and roof of the casemate are earthed
over, with an opening at the front and rear. The remaining casemates are about
35 feet by 36 feet, and consist of the gun-compartment only. Arc of fire of the guns
in casemates 90° – 120° .
Accommodation: Underground concrete shelters.
Observation: Possible OP's at 138789 and 161793.
Secondary Armament: One to three light AA guns.
Dummy: At 153772, occupied by dummy guns with split trails.

Formation of P-51D Mustangs of the 361st Fighter Group at Bottisham, Cambridgeshire with invasion stripes applied to the wings and fuselages.

Douglas A-20 43-10129 of the 416th Bomb Group on fire from a flak hit on 12 May when the US 9th Air Force carried out 'Eagle', a full-scale exercise of the tactics and techniques of paradrop, glider tow, parapack in resupply, air landing of supplies and medical evacuation as a dress rehearsal for the airborne invasion of Normandy .

Opposite page: Happy American glider pilots being returned to England after flying paratroopers to their objectives. British glider pilots were organized as ground troops in a special glider pilot regiment but the American glider pilots were simply an element within the troop carrier squadrons.

Commandant Philippe Kieffer who commanded two troops of French Fusiliers Marins and a light machine gun platoon (177 men).

Opposite page: A British soldier armed with a Bren gun beside a Horsa glider which came to rest near a wall.

Oberstleutnant Josef 'Pips' Priller, Kommodore, Jagdgeschwader 26. When Priller and his regular Kacmarek (wingman), Unteroffizier Heinz Wodarczyk attacked 'Sword' Beach six German prisoners took advantage of the situation and tried to bolt but Kieffer's' men promptly mowed them down.

'This is IT! D-Day! Invasion!

Opposite page: At 0630 on D-Day three companies (225 men) of the 2nd Ranger Battalion (Force 'A') using rocket propelled grapple hooks attached to climbing ropes and portable extension ladders scaled the cliffs within ten minutes after landing to capture the position at the Pointe-du-Hoc.

Lieutenant Colonel James Earl Rudder, a 34-year old college teacher and football coach from Brady, Texas who led the assault by the 2nd Ranger Battalion on Pointe du Hoc, even though Lieutenant General Clarence Huebner had forbidden him to do so.

Rangers at the battery at Pointe du Hoc after it was taken in the assault up the cliffs. By 8 June, 2nd Ranger casualties were; 135 killed, wounded and missing - a casualty rate of 60 per cent.

was going to be vital because it was going to be placed outside the wire which would 'illuminate the area very quickly so that the three gliders bound for the battery would see where to land. One machine gun, a Vickers, had arrived, fortunately. But worst of all there were no Royal Engineers with special explosives with which to destroy the guns. We hadn't got much in the way of explosives, every two men carried parts of a Gammon bomb, a bag with explosive mainly for use against tanks, but that wasn't much really.'

Lieutenant Alan Jefferson, 9th Battalion, Parachute Regiment who had been detailed to lead the assault on the first of the four gun bunkers known as Number One Casemate. A former ballet dancer, on the occasional weekends off while under training for the operation he had gone to London to spend time with Lisa Grogan who was appearing in *Swan Lake* **at the People's Palace Theatre in the Mile End Road.**

'Intelligence indicated that the Merville battery contained four 155mm calibre guns, each capable of bombarding the landing beaches and 160 men in 15-20 weapons pits, each with 4-5 machine guns and possibly three 20mm anti-aircraft guns. (In fact 130 men of the 1716th Artillery Regiment commanded by Leutnant Raimund Steiner who were billeted nearby in Franceville-Plâge and Gonneville-en-Auge manned the battery, which consisted of four Czechoslovakian 10cm LFH 14/19 field howitzers on wheels, made by Skoda, with a range of four miles). The guns were in four steel-doored concrete emplacements built of 6 feet of reinforced concrete, two of which were also covered by 12 feet of earth. They were in a fenced area of 700 by 500 yards within which was a belt of barbed wire, double in places, 15 feet thick and five feet high. A 400-yard anti-tank ditch, 15 feet wide by 10 feet deep around two sides was incomplete but mines had been sown profusely and there were a dual-purpose gun position and about fifteen weapon pits. Outside the main position was a wired in strong-point with five machine-gun emplacements and several other anti-aircraft gun positions. The 9th Battalion prepared with several rehearsals on a full size mock-up of the Battery built specially at a farm at West Woodhay near Newbury.

A 750 strong assault force was to land on a DZ 1¼ miles east of the battery after 'C' Company, 1st Canadian Parachute Battalion had captured and secured the DZ and Pathfinder Paras of the 22nd Independent Parachute Company had marked it. 'A' Company, 1st Canadian Parachute Battalion was to protect the left flank of the 9th Battalion in its approach march and attack on the Battery. It was planned to land the paratroops and sappers in eleven gliders who would clear and mark paths through the minefields before the main assault was launched. A glider assault party of three Horsa gliders, ferrying three officers and 47 OR (other ranks) of 'A' Company, plus one officer and seven OR of the 591st Parachute Squadron Royal Engineers, who carried explosives to destroy the guns, were to land within the Battery perimeter itself.

The first group were dropped accurately at 0020 but the C-47 Dakotas carrying the Canadians dropped over a wide area and only about 30 Canadians landed on the DZ. Pilots of the 32 Dakotas carrying the main body (around 540 paras) were hampered by a huge dust cloud caused by the RAF bombing raid and poor visibility caused by patchy cloud and a strong easterly wind. Almost all the Battalion and much of the Brigade were scattered over a wide area, many landing in the flooded fields. In Otway's C-47 only 7 of the 20 men managed to jump while over the DZ and the Dakota had to make three more runs to get them all out. Otway landed beside a German HQ, which fired at him. The firing only ceased when a para threw a brick through the window and the enemy obviously thought it was a grenade! Also, the gliders carrying the mortars, anti-tank guns, mine detectors and all the heavy equipment landed well to the south east and Otway's only heavy equipment was now a solitary Vickers machine gun.

By 0250 only about 150 paras were grouped together. No support could be expected from the glider borne troops either. One of the three Horsas broke its tow rope just after take-off and had to make an emergency landing at RAF Odiham. The second landed several miles east of the battery and the third flew over the battery and crashed in an orchard about 100 yards away to the south west having been hit by AA fire.

Meanwhile, the advance party had cut the outer wire fence but the lack of mine detectors and tape meant that a path through had been achieved by searching for them with bare hands and making them safe one by one. To mark the path they had dragged their feet to scratch two lines in the earth. Otway reorganized his men into seven parties. Two were to breach the main wire, four were to deal with the four guns and one was to make a diversion at the main entrance. At this juncture two of the Albemarles appeared and flew around looking for the place to crash land. It had not been possible to put out lights to guide them, but eventually the gliders were released, landing 200 yards away. Their troops engaged the Germans in the perimeter defences. Gaps were blown in the wire and the paras stormed the battery. The diversion party attacked through the main gate and hand-to-hand fighting ensued for 20 minutes until the Germans finally capitulated. 22 prisoners were taken and at 0445 the success signal was fired. (HMS *Arethusa* was standing by to pound the battery with her 6-inch guns at 0550 if the attack failed). The 75 paras still standing left for high ground around Amfreville; taking their wounded with them. Later in the day the 736th Grenadier Regiment re-occupied the Battery and a message was received by Major-General Richard Gale stating that 'the guns had opened fire'. Next day Nos. 4 and 5 Troops, 3 Commando assaulted the Battery and the defenders were overcome, but the enemy counter-attacked using self-propelled guns and drove the commandos out.

* * *

'I landed about a mile and a quarter from the battery, up to my neck in a ditch. When I climbed out I met a surprised Frenchman and then the 150 of us met up in a wood. A major problem was the lack of any tape used to mark paths through minefields. It meant we had to feel our way in single file, on hands and knees, most of the way there. I sometimes wonder if the Germans were waiting. It wasn't until the Bangalore torpedoes went in that all hell broke loose. Up to then there was almost total silence. It was uncanny. There was this almighty clatter. I'm sure it must have come from their 20mm gun. I was half way there, running like hell across the open ground within sight of the target with my Sten and just folded up in the air and came down on my back.

Sergeant Percy Reeve.

'I saw an Airedale terrier standing in a section of barbed wire. A corporal told me not to touch it because it was stuffed and booby trapped because the Germans knew the British like dogs... There was a lot of hand-to-hand fighting and a terrific amount of small arms fire. We were coming under fire from what I think were 88s. I pressed on to No.4 Casement to the left of the main road where a dead German was lying near the entrance. I went inside and saw a gun, which was a lot smaller than the 150s we had anticipated. I said we could get rid of it with some grenades in the ammunition nearby but before this could go ahead, there was a bang and all I could remember was my back had been ripped open and my legs were twitching. I thought I'd bought it. I remember calling for my mum - it was my 21st birthday. I felt that bad that I actually asked Paddy Jenkins to finish me off. Then Sid Capon came in... I got up and found I could walk a few steps and he sort of carried me out of the Casement. They sat George Hawkins up in there and he kept shouting, 'Don't leave us. Don't leave us. [Hawkins was too badly wounded to be moved]. Then a couple of chaps came up with a bit of door. They carried me a little way on that and then once we got outside the wire some boys came along with this handcart. There was already another boy on there and they laid me on there and got me outside the Battery as far as we could go and then left me with Major Bestley.'

Private Alan Mower.

'None of us is going to die. We're all brave men. We're not going to die. 'Twenty minutes to go, lads! Equipment check!' Each man would check the equipment of the man in front of him, his chute, etc and each chute would be on to the strongpoint. It didn't seem long, those twenty minutes. Then, 'We're approaching the coast!' And as we approached the coast of France the German ack-ack came up at us. You could see the amber glows.

'I had a beautiful landing, the best ever landing I've ever had. I landed in a field right near a hedgerow with a road running parallel and a dwelling opposite. I wasn't interested in the dwelling. You were always taught: 'There's only one objective. No private battles'. I released my chute. I felt most dejected: there was nobody around. I saw the plane go round, along and away and all of a sudden another parachute came down about two or three yards from me. We took the cover of the hedgerow and then we met another chap and off we went; three of us now and carried on another hundred yards and we met Lieutenant Dowling from 'B' Company. He had about six people with him and he was trying to find his bearings and was slaying these stinging nettles. A lorry came along with some Germans on it but we hid in the hedgerow, not forgetting: 'No private warfare.'

20-year old Private Sidney Capon, a popular Londoner in the 9th Battalion, Parachute Regiment.

'The moon was coming and going behind clouds and we had our first sight of the casements, looking like toads squatting there, somehow nasty and we came to the outside wire. The bombing of the battery had not disturbed the casements at all but it had made enormous craters, so you had enormous depths and heights of earth and it had been raining and it was greyish and wet and nasty and sticky. I got my little party together and gave them a little pep talk. 'We're here, we've trained for it; we're ready for it. If we don't do it, imagine what will happen to your wives and daughters' and so on.

'We were waiting for the gliders and then we saw the first glider. It came from the north-west and did a kind of circle and whistled as it went over and disappeared. In front of us was an ack-ack gun on a concrete block, it hadn't spoken and then a few moments later another glider came - this was Hugh Pond's - and this gun opened up, a little clip of five rounds and five balls of fire shot up. The glider seemed to pause, looking, searching and then another five got nearer and then the next five and one hit it. There was a flash and the tail of the glider was on fire.'

Lieutenant Alan Jefferson, 9th Battalion, Parachute Regiment.

'The plan involved landing three gliders in the gaps between the casemates. In addition to the arrester parachute, the wings of the gliders would snap off on hitting the casemates stopping the glider more quickly than usual. The Battalion would parachute in ahead of us on a DZ about a mile and a half away. As the gliders crash-landed inside the Battery, the Battalion would be assaulting from the outside. I was twenty years old, had never been in battle before and was tremendously excited at the prospect.

'We took off at about midnight. I was up front behind the pilots. We had six sappers whose job was to blow the guns. One of my chaps had a flame-thrower. Over the Battery we were hot by light anti-aircraft fire. The first shots exploded outside the glider and all we heard were distant thumps, which didn't really worry us. We knew what they were but it didn't bother us. But then we were actually hit by four or five small anti-aircraft shells, one of which, unfortunately, set fire to the flame-thrower. So in the last minute, the last few seconds, the glider was on fire and one of the unfortunate chaps was of course on fire. We swooped in, we did see the battery - both Sergeant Kerr and I shouted at the same time, 'There's the battery!' - but then immediately a very large barbed wire entanglement loomed up in front. Sergeant Kerr pulled up the rudder, we shot over the fence and the glider crash-landed in an orchard about 150 yards outside the battery. There was a facility for breaking the glider in half with explosives - it was lined with explosives in the middle and you pulled a wire and set it off - but there was no need because the crash-landing had broken the glider in half and the wings were off. By this time this poor chap must have been dead with the flames and we all rushed out of the gap in the glider as quickly as we could. It was all confusion.

We heard noises in the opposite direction and realised that they must be Germans coming up a narrow lane. We jumped into the ditch and engaged them. After a while as it was getting light, the firing died down. I heard a shot behind us and there coming through a minefield was the Battalion Physical Training Instructor. We shouted, 'Go back. It's a minefield'

'No its not, it's a dummy; you're to rejoin the Battalion'; he replied.

'This was our first contact with the Battalion.'

Lieutenant Hubert Pond 9th Battalion, Parachute Regiment.

'The third glider never arrived. That landed back in England, the towrope broke. So there were no gliders and it now came that we had to attack the guns. Otway turned round and said we'd got to attack now. 'Get ready, men,' he says. Then, 'Get in! Get in!'

'There were about seven men, instead of thirty-two, to attack No 1 gun. Jefferson fell down wounded. We carried on zigzagging and I shouted, as I did in training, *'Bastards! Bastards! Bastards!'* and I heard shouts and explosions from my left, No 2 gun and shouts of 'Mines!' It was very, very quick. Don't forget, you're rushing in. I never saw Mike Dowling again. He was killed.

'We reached the rear of No 1 gun, still on our feet, four of us. We threw two grenades into the lobby and there were noises from inside the casement and the Germans pushed themselves out the rear and I remember one or two of them shouting, *Russki! Russki!* and I thought, *'What the hell are they on about, Russki! Russki!?'* But by all accounts they were Russians made to fight for the Germans. The last chappy was a big chap, he wore glasses and he was in a terrible state. He was on his hands and knees.'

Private Sidney Capon 9th Battalion, Parachute Regiment. Mike Dowling was a close friend of Alan Jefferson. They shared the same sense of humour and revelled about the risk of stepping on a land mine at Merville. They both agreed that after the war farming seemed a good occupation and they even talked about a joint venture abroad, possibly growing oranges. Once Dowling had completed his mission he had reported to Colonel Otway who asked him if he was sure that all the guns had been put out of action. Dowling said that he would personally go back and examine them but as he ran shells began to fall, some detonating landmines buried near the casements. Suddenly, there as an explosion and the blast killed Dowling instantly. (Leutnant Raimund Steiner in his command bunker had asked the Houlgate Battery further east to shell his Battery knowing that his men would be safe in their casements but that the attackers would be killed in the open. However, Otway had set everyone to work to carry the wounded to a barn beyond the minefield. Among the German survivors was an elderly doctor and he started with impartial care to attend to the worst of the wounded, both British and German. Before long, both British and German medical supplies in the barn were finished. The German doctor knew where extra supplies had

been stored in the battery and he set off alone through the fire to fetch them. On the way he was killed by a German shell). Alan Jefferson was one of 22 men (with two captured German orderlies) left at a farmhouse near the Merville battery when Otway's remaining soldiers headed southwest towards the village of Le Plein, the next objective, 2 miles away. Jefferson and one of the German orderlies looked in vain for Dowling's body for 45 minutes before giving up.

'We were about two minutes away from the drop zone when we ran into heavy flak. During the run-in the pilots of the transports took all sorts of evasive action. 9th Para were scattered all over the place. Unfortunately though we were dropped in the right place between two rivers, at 10 past midnight, we didn't know that the Germans had flooded the area in three feet of water. There were posts in the ground and coils of barbed wire. It was quite a shock and we lost many men drowned when they got caught up in wire. I was lucky; I was right on the edge but I got sodden wet. I managed to get clear and, with the help of a prismatic compass, which was thankfully waterproof, I made my way to the rendezvous.

'We all made for the RV, picking up individual people on the way. We weren't at all nervous. We were professionals. Every soldier was reliable. I never thought for a moment that we'd fail. We were positive about everything; you just got on with it. Of course we were all fully aware of the dangers and the possibility we might be killed at any time but we never gave it a second thought.

'We had to head up through fields and hedgerows. It took us three hours to cover three miles because we could not afford to be seen or be heard. Surprise was everything. On the way I saw one of the gliders that had crashed. On a road we saw two Germans on bicycles but we let them go on. It would have been fatal if they knew we were there.

'At the RV I was reasonably happy. I had three quarters of the platoon, about 15 men. We waited till we got the OK to go in. No one spoke. It was total silence. Although we had fewer men we would still carry out the attacks on each casement. Colonel Otway simply said, 'Go to it!' As soon as the Bangalore torpedoes went off I headed for No.2 casement as quickly as possible. The faster the better. We had eight minutes to do the job and get out. Sergeant Sid Knight and his party of about eight headed for the main gate and I followed on behind them. On the way we passed Colonel Otway standing on the edge of the perimeter. He shouted, 'Get those bloody machine gunners!' I was a trained sniper and I carried a shortened Lee Enfield rifle with telescopic sights. The German machine gunner was about 150 yards away. I looked through the sight and fired a shot between the 12-inch-opening at the front of the machine gunner's concrete bunker. (Even if the bullet missed, the ricochet inside would probably kill him). He didn't fire anymore.

'I carried on to No.2 casement and reached the top where I dropped a Mill's grenade down one of the chimney pipes. Several Germans came out with their hands up. They looked old and dirty. They were handed over to the REs.

'Surprise, as far as I was concerned, was total. What efficiency! Two years training and all over in 8-10 minutes! From there we had to make haste to the LZ to meet the gliders coming in.

'Though the big guns weren't there we prevented a bloodbath on the beach.'

Sniper John Walker, platoon Sergeant, 9th Battalion, Parachute Regiment. A Norfolk territorial before the war, he had celebrated his 22nd birthday a week before D-Day.

'The actual boys and myself, the average age was 19 to 21. No older. Our officers were a bit older. Our NCOs were a bit older, because 'Windy' (General Gale) had nicked a lot of NCOs from the 1st Division who had experience to put in amongst us so as to give us that bit of backing and a bit of experience. Anyway, the first thing we knew about this was we knew something was up, 'cos if you remember we had these little exercises and it always seemed to be guns we were after - up the hill and down the valley and then one day a little while before Normandy they marched us out and we stopped at the Battalion and the Colonel told us what the job was. Well after that we went down on the plains and the Colonel found a position practically like this (the Merville Battery) and we built a battery and we attacked it night and day for a week. The idea was that first of all to drop would be our pathfinders, then some of the lads would drop and they'd make for the battery, make sure it was alright and then we get to the RV and we do the approach march which was approximately about a mile and a half across the fields. And then when we got here we had three gliders coming in with twenty paras in each who had volunteered to go in, those gliders, to actually crash land in the battery when we put the attack in. That was at the same time that one party came up here to the main gate. They would attack from that position. Well we were to come through and blow the wire in four positions. 'C' Company was the attacking Company. Then once through those four positions we had to take a gun each and blow it. And everything we done just dovetailed and it was beautiful. We were so confident that we could do it, he'd brainwashed us too much. So anyway, a couple of weeks' later, three o'clock in the morning, lights go on in the barrack room. 'Right - get up; get your kit - OUT'. And when we walked out on the square there were all these transporters. Into the transporters and I think we drove around for about 8 hours, changing drivers here and there and the last thing we knew there was all these tanks, all the barbed wire round it. In we went; they shut the gate and said, 'You stay there'. And we'd had a big mosaic made of the battery itself and we had to study that and an officer could stop you any time and say, 'Where is so-and-so in the battery?' And if you didn't know, mate, you were back in there and you were stuck in there an hour and you had to explain everything to him. So everybody knew exactly what the other chap was doing and exactly what was in there and it looked a perfect plan. But come the night, 5 June, we took off just after midnight and we dropped just before one.

'It was a beautiful flight across till we hit the coast and we hit the coast and you've never seen anything like it in your life. It was just like going into a firework display and the old duck was going five ways at once and everybody was saying, 'Let's get out of this so-and-so thing'. Anyway eventually the pilot says, 'Go' and puts the light on and on our way we go. And as I dropped, obviously you look round and I could see other 'chutes coming down and I hit the deck and out of my 'chute, got my Sten out, everything going, look round - couldn't see anybody. But there was one thing that got implanted in my mind - we must get to that RV. And the Colonel's orders were 'You are to have no private fire fights. You get to the RV AND THAT IS IT'. And I checked around a bit. I found the road that runs in front of the rendezvous. I didn't know which way to go - right or left - but I heard a fire fight going on up to the left so I thought I'd go up to the right. And I just got along the side of the road looking and away in the distance I could just see this red light twinkling. And it was one of the officers got up the tree with an Aldis lamp and was flicking this right round in circles to bring the lads in. As soon as I saw that I knew where I was to get. I could see the tree across the fields and I saw a bod just in front of where I knew the RV was and I yelled the password out and he yelled it back and I looked at him and it was the Colonel. He was standing there waiting to bring the lads in. He tapped me on the shoulder and he said, 'Well done, lad. What company?' 'C' Company.' 'Down there.' I went down there and... I dropped down beside my Lieutenant (Jackson) and had a little word with him, you know. At the time I thought, well there don't seem many of us here, but you know most of us thought that but we didn't say it. 'Cos there's 100 of us in the company. It didn't look 100, but you didn't say anything because you didn't want to upset anybody. Any rate we were sitting there and we knew the timetable, knew we ought to be moving now. We ought to be moving and eventually the Colonel said 'Move' and it wasn't until years afterwards I found out that out of the 550 who jumped in our battalion, only 150 got to the rendezvous.'

Paratrooper Les Cartwright, 9th Parachute Battalion who dropped for the Merville Battery.

'In the distance the intermittent sounds of machine-gun fire could be heard, while close at hand the groans and bellowings of injured cattle and fresh bomb craters, bore witness to the bombings of two hours before. Near Gonneville-en-Auge, they froze suddenly, as a patrol of twenty Germans crossed the track twenty-five metres ahead of them and then, with sighs of relief, they continued their advance. A small scouting party had landed in advance of the battalion. At the road junction near the battery, just past Gonneville, the party met the oncoming troops. They reported that the bombing attack had missed the battery.'

Red Berets into Normandy **by Captain Huw Wheldon of the 6th Airborne Division. Later, Sir Hugh Wheldon became Managing Director of BBC Television.**

'My orders were to take a diversionary party of six men around the perimeter and make a noisy break-in at the main gate while the rest carried out a main assault through the breaches in the perimeter. I actually dropped quite a way off target because when I'd gone to jump my harness had somehow hooked on to a handle on the door leading to the pilot's cabin. I'd hammered on the door, which opened and set me loose, but this delay of a few seconds meant that I landed in a field full of cows.

'Suddenly these Lancasters started dropping their 4,000-pounders around me, so I was bouncing up and down in a ditch. As these bombs were coming down and the cows were being blown to bits, I suddenly thought of this old Cadbury's advert, which said, 'Where is your chocolate?' I thought, 'It's with a soldier alone in an unfriendly country!'

'Anyway, things became a bit quieter after the bombs dropped, so I made my way round to the rendezvous. The planning was so good that when I dropped I knew where I was immediately. The first bloke I saw was Sergeant Salter, so we ran together to the rendezvous. When I arrived, there was hardly anyone there at all. Then one of my old mates turned up plus a few more. My diversionary party was attached to Headquarters Company so we were given orders to do what we could, but we had no weapons. I had just one pistol, one Bren gunner and one Sten in my party. Anyway, Colonel Otway then decided that we'd go off to the battery and do our job there.

'It was very dark and we all went through the lanes from the rendezvous at Varaville to the Merville battery. When we got near to the battery, everybody had his job to do. We numbered about 150; that's all. At the battery we found Major Alan Parry with the battery reconnaissance party: I was close to the Colonel and Hal Hudson the adjutant all the time.

'There was hardly any noise whatsoever and the battery loomed out of the darkness. You could see the outlines of the four big guns facing the sea. We'd come over the barbed wire and there was an old perimeter track leading up to the battery so I started to make a movement around this road when machine-guns opened up from both sides. Someone shouted out, 'Get those bloody machine guns!' I had only one man with me and I took his Sten gun from him. We found there were three guns, one outside and two inside the perimeter, in front of No. 1 battery. I got the bloke on the outside corner by the forming-up point and then we went into the battery. It was very dark, but I could see that one of the gunners was by a whacking great lump of concrete that had been blown up. His tracer gave him away, so I got right round behind him and put my gun on him, which soon quietened him.

'I had a go at the third one. Whether I got him or not I don't know, but it all went quiet. I went back to report to the Colonel and was just going towards the actual objective when I saw Major Parry on the right-hand side of the track wounded in the leg. On the left side was Captain Hudson and he had a terrible wound in his stomach - I think a shell must have hit him. I carried on with my diversionary party inside the perimeter and as we reached the main gate, we saw some Germans walking in, waving white flags. A couple of our blokes were shouting out, 'Shoot them.' Of course, I shouted, 'You can't shoot them - they've got the white flag up,' and so we rounded them up. I went and had a look in the batteries myself. Some chaps put two shells in the gun - one at the breech and one in the barrel! When the gun fired, the shells blew one another and the gun to pieces, I did not see the actual firing but I heard the explosions.

'The 12th Battalion were ordered to attack Bréville to relieve us. You could look down on them and actually see the battle taking place with our boys attacking. They relieved us tremendously by doing that and then they took Bréville. The ridge was held and the Germans didn't contest it again. Marvellous job. I don't think I'd be here today if they hadn't done that. They lost an awful lot of men, though, some killed by our own gunfire. We then moved up to the crossroads at Le Mesnil and my little party dug in at the brickworks. Of course, the Jerries had a fixed line on it, so as soon as we got into the brickworks, boom, boom, down came the shells and RSM Cunningham was hit. We picked him up and called the medics and put him in the ambulance. He looked at me and said, 'I'll tell you this, when we get back to barracks, I'll remember who the real soldiers were.' I said, 'All right, Bill, you get yourself better.' Later the medics came back and I asked, 'How is the RSM?' They said, 'He's gone.' Terrible waste because Le Mesnil was our last place to go before being relieved.'

Company Sergeant-Major Sid Knight, 9th Parachute Battalion.

'By five o'clock we had completely occupied the battery. We had taken all the casements, we had taken twenty-two prisoners and there were a lot of German casualties, killed and wounded, in the casements and I was able to send a success signal. I had no radio to send a success signal but I lit a yellow signal flare and an RAF plane went over, saw it and waggled its wings. And my signals officer, unbeknown to me, had got a carrier pigeon with him, brought it all the way from England in his airborne smock and he tied a victory message around its leg and sent it off.

'Then the problem was to get out. I went round the casements and I told all the troops to get out but we didn't know how to get through the minefield so I told the prisoners to show me the way. They refused. So I said, 'Well, OK, we're going to make you walk forward and if you don't show us the way through the mines we're just going to start shooting the ground and you're going to lose your feet and maybe the mines will go up too.' So they showed us the way and we got out.

'I went and sat by the calvary [roadside crucifix] near the battery and I told everybody to take up defensive positions such as we were able to do. Because, out of the 150 men that we went in with, all ranks, there were only 75 of us left standing on our feet. The others had been killed or wounded.'

Lieutenant Colonel Terence Otway, CO, 9th Battalion, Parachute Regiment.

'We felt we'd done a grand job. But afterwards you think, 'My God, what's happened to all the guys?' And you start looking round to see who's left.

Like in all regiments, you have a certain circle of fairly close people you know fairly well and so it was in the 9th Battalion that that circle was really the old Essex Regiment, where we'd been together for two years, three years, up to that time. There might have been hundreds of people that you didn't even know, not personally, put it that way; but then there's another hundred or so that you did know quite personally, especially a lot of the NCOs, because we were all young NCOs together. And then you thought, 'My God, where's he gone?' And that's the only time it really hit you, to think, 'I was bloody lucky to get out of that.' Something you don't think about when you're going in.'

Company Sergeant-Major Barney Ross, 9th Battalion, Parachute Regiment.

'The colonel was sitting on the steps of this calvary, writing or talking and scattered around were troops looking pretty worn and torn. There were a lot of wounded on stretchers and there were stretcher-bearers moving around. They all claimed that the attack was a great success but they had had to get a move on, because, without a success signal from us, the cruiser Arethusa was going to fire on the battery with its six-inch guns. I think the attack put the battery out for a certain amount of time but the battery was never completely put out of operation. I think the plan was as near perfect as could be, but never, ever, ever has any battle gone according to plan. You just cannot foresee the chaos that is going to ensue. The 9th Battalion were the people trained to get in there and do the job and they did the best they could. They'd lost most of their equipment. They tried to wreck the guns; they weren't engineers, they did not wreck the guns. They broke a few things. They hadn't been trained to remove the sights; they hadn't been trained to do anything. They threw grenades into the bunkers and through every air vent but they didn't have time to go down and see if there were many left. They knew that the cruiser was going to open fire and if they didn't move off they were all going to be killed, so they went.

'Luckily the guns were very small guns. They were not the 150-millimetres which everybody had said; they were only very, very ancient 75-millimetre guns of Czech manufacture, so although the guns did continue to fire they were not very effective because their calibre was so small. In fact the Germans did not give up that battery until they were told to withdraw when Montgomery's 21st Army Group started to advance. So although it has been made a battle honour of the regiment and it was a glorious thing and I think for a lot of men a tremendously brave thing to do, it didn't really have the outcome on the battle that we thought it would.'

Lieutenant Hubert Pond, 9th Battalion, Parachute Regiment. After the paras had left Leutnant Steiner inspected his guns and discovered that they were in a better condition than he expected and at least one could be fired by gunners once they arrived from another unit nearby. While Otway's men attacked Le Plein, Steiner returned to his control bunker and at 1600 hours he ordered his men to aim their fire at the lock on the Caen Canal. Steiner's father, known to be anti-Nazi, was to die of ill-

treatment in a concentration camp. On the morning of 7 June the battery was attacked again, by two troops of 3 Commando commanded by Major John Pooley. Losses on both sides were heavy and the major was among the dad. The Merville Battery was finally silenced by the RAF and the guns of the Royal Navy.

'Having captured the battery, the battalion, now reduced to eighty of all ranks, moved on to carry out its second task, the seizure of some high ground near Le Plein. On approaching the village of Hauger, the Commanding Officer was warned by a Frenchman that 200 of the enemy were there entrenched ready to dispute his arrival. Almost immediately afterwards battle was joined. It was by now full daylight and Otway could see that the main opposition offered by the enemies came from one particular house. It was attacked by thirty men, but since it was loop-holed for defence and surrounded by a wall six feet high, it proved too strong to be taken. In point of fact, the garrison of the village was composed for the most part of Russians forced to fight by the Germans and informed that if they fell alive into the hands of the Allies they would be shot as traitors. This in all probability accounts for the strength of the resistance offered. The battalion was not strong enough to capture the feature immediately and therefore went to ground and suffered much from snipers; but, when it had been reinforced the next afternoon by the 1st Special Service Brigade, the village was successfully cleared.

By Air To Battle: The Official Account of the British Airborne Divisions.

Chapter 4

The Pointe

'We took off at about 2am and had a leisurely flight down England to the south coast and across the Channel to the Normandy coast flying between 6-7,000 feet. There was low cloud most of the way but it started to break up as we approached France. I still did not know whether the Allied Forces would land. But about five miles out from the coast, when I could just discern the dark grey surface of the sea beneath in the early twilight, the fleet of invasion barges right below opened their throttles for the dash to the beach. It was too dark for me to see the boats but their increased speed made white wakes and these showed up clearly. I knew it was 'on'. Some of the wakes were all over the place. There must have been a few collisions at that level. Undoubtedly it was the most thrilling and emotional experience for me in all the years of the war. Until that moment Bomber Command had alone been taking the war to the Germans. For all I knew it would continue on and on until my crew and I finally joined the killed-in-action list. A massive army on the continent meant it was not unreasonable to think that the war might finish and I might get to see Grace and Sue (wife and daughter) again. The battery was well marked by the Pathfinders and from a relatively low height, about 6,500 feet. We all took our time, each aircraft dropping 13,000lbs of bombs. The whole Pointe was battered; the battery including its concrete bunkers was destroyed. Even a part of the cliff tumbled into the sea. US soldiers [2nd Ranger Battalion], who about two hours later (had they been on time they would have seen and heard us), scaled the cliff to attack and silence the guns not knowing of our attack. They reported the shambles of shattered concrete and steel they saw when they reached the top.'

Wing Commander Rollo Kingsford-Smith RAAF the Australian CO of 463 Squadron RAAF, which was equipped with Avro Lancasters; a nephew of Sir Charles Kingsford-Smith MC [17]

'During the navigators' pre-briefing, I received all the maps and general instructions concerning flak batteries, and I was told that our target was a 16 inch gun on the coast near Pointe-du-Hoc that was encased in tons of concrete on a hillside. Briefing for all crews for the first D-Day mission was at 2300 hours, and during the briefing we heard General Eisenhower tell us that we were embarking on a 'Great Crusade.'

'H-hour was scheduled for 06:30 when the Higgins boats, with just two feet of draft, were to land. After we bombed, the 2nd Ranger Battalion was

17   Charles Kingsford-Smith MC who with fellow pilot C. T. P. Ulm and crew made the first Trans-Pacific flight 31 May-9 June 1928 in Fokker F.VIIB/3m Southern Cross.

Pointe-du-Hoc Timeline

Allied intelligence pinpointed 73 fixed coastal gun batteries that could menace the invasion. At Pointe-du-Hoc, a cliff rising 100 feet high from a very rocky beach, 3.7 miles west of Vierville, a six-gun battery (thought to be 155mm, with a range of 25,000 yards) could engage ships at sea and fire directly onto 'Utah' and 'Omaha'. The gun positions were bombed throughout May, with a heavier than average attack by both day and night three days before D-Day and then again during the night of 5 June. Then, at 0630 three companies (225 men) of the 2nd Ranger Battalion (Force 'A') using rocket propelled grapple hooks attached to climbing ropes and portable extension ladders were to scale the cliffs within ten minutes after landing and capture the position. The assault on the Pointe-du-Hoc was to have been led by a recently promoted executive officer who managed to get himself 'thoroughly drunk' while still aboard his transport in Weymouth harbour. The drunken officer was sent ashore and hospitalized and he was 'never seen again'. Lieutenant Colonel James Earl Rudder, a 34-year old college teacher and football coach from Brady, Texas decided he would lead the assault, even though Lieutenant General Clarence Huebner had forbidden him to do so. 'I'm sorry to have to disobey you sir' Rudder had replied 'but if I don't take it, it might not go.'

Company 'C', 2nd Ranger Battalion meanwhile, was to scale the bluffs of Pointe-de-la-Percée, 1¼ mile NW of Vierville. Lieutenant Colonel Maxwell Schneider's 5th Ranger Battalion and the 2nd Battalion's 'A' and 'B' Companies constituted Force 'C', reinforcement, which were to wait offshore. If Schneider did not receive a signal by H+30 he was to land his men on 'Omaha' and proceed overland through Pointe-de-la-Percée to attack Pointe-du-Hoc. (Schneider's men were not called upon so they moved four miles east, to Dog White, where they spearheaded the advance off the bloody beach and had captured Vierville by evening).

At Pointe-du-Hoc, in addition to the main concrete emplacements, many of which connected by tunnels or protected walkways, there were trenches and machine gun posts constructed around the perimeter fences and the cliff edge. The garrison numbered about 200 men of the static 716th Coastal Defence Division, mostly non-Germans. In anticipation of commando landings, 240 mm shells attached to trip wires had been placed at 100 yards intervals along the cliff. The fortifications came under heavy fire by *Texas* from H-40 minutes to H-05 minutes and 18 medium bombers hit the German positions just before the Rangers (who were 40 minutes late) arrived. But when the sea bombardment had been lifted according to schedule and when the Rangers landed, the Germans had filtered back into the fortifications and were waiting for them with machine-guns, rifles and hand-grenades, which they rolled down the cliffs.

0550-0625 From 10 miles off shore USS *Texas* fired about 600 14-inch shells at the six-gun battery at Pointe-du-Hoc overlooking both 'Omaha' and 'Utah' beaches before changing targets to shell the resistance nests at 'Omaha'.

0610 A last minute strike is made on the Pointe-du-Hoc by 18 medium bombers.

0708 2nd Ranger Battalion lands to begin scaling the cliffs leading to the battery but they arrive 40 minutes later than scheduled and from a direction parallel with the coast, having been misdirected to Pointe-de-la-Percée nearby, which allows the battery garrison to spot them and open fire with small arms and 20 mm flak.

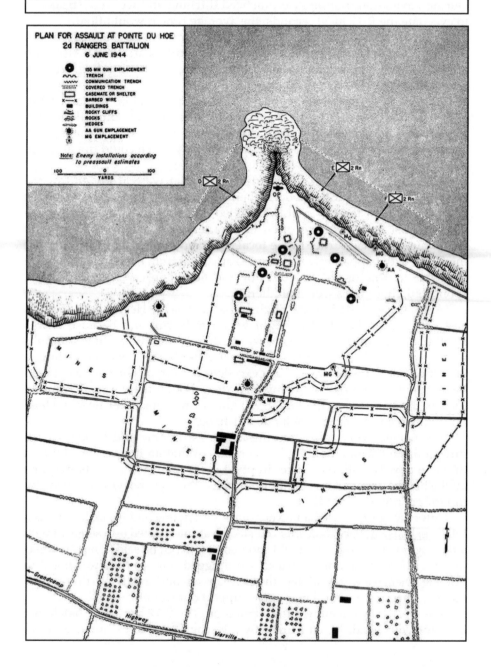

scheduled to use steel hooks to scale the 100 foot cliff to get to the 150 mm gun if we failed to take it out.

'The Colonel told us that there was no place to ditch, so all pilots were to make sure that they could make it to France and back before heading over the Channel. Ordinarily, if you had trouble getting back to the base you could ditch in the Channel, usually nose up and air-sea rescue would pick you up from your last position, after you gave a 'Mayday Mayday' signal. During navigation training, we practiced ditching and we were supposed to evacuate the B-17 in 30 seconds, the average time it would float.

'We were also told during briefing that 'Guns will be manned but not test fired. Gunners will not fire at any planes unless attacked.' Also, 'No secondary runs will be made on any primary target.' After briefing, we took the jitney to our plane.

'It was a very epic occasion but a very routine mission. We took off at 02:19 and we assembled over Buncher 10 to 20,000 feet. Our pilots, Dan Houghton and Julian 'Tex' Carr took us up in an old plane named *Quarterback*. Our objective was a German battery, which could fire as much as 13 miles off shore.

'The take-off was over four or five trees that were at the end of the runway, which was another story. When we took off with bomb loads about one-third heavier than normal, we needed the whole runway to just make it over those trees and we often hit the leaves. I believe that Colonel Goodman had gone earlier to the local constabulary to ask if we could cut them down, but apparently you needed approval from the crown. When we returned to Knettishall in 2003 for the 60th anniversary tour that I sponsored, those trees were still there.

'At 03:58 we headed for the English coast at Beachy Head, about 15 miles east of Brighton beach. The flight was a milk run and because it was 10/10ths undercover, the targets were attacked by PFF methods. Bombs were away at 06:56 hours from 15,050 feet. After bombs away, according to the official mission statement, 'An excellent pattern of release was noted.' We encountered no flak or enemy aircraft, although there were 25 ground rockets fired at us near the target. All aircraft returned over Beachy Head for letdown and landing.' We landed at 10:00.

'I remember very well standing at the astrodome and looking in all directions and seeing nothing but contrails. What an impressive sight. In that one day, The 8th Air Force dropped more tonnage in two hours than all the bombs dropped on Hamburg in 1943 - the most heavily bombed city in Europe in World War II.

'After we returned we had a very quick de-briefing and we all hit the sack totally exhausted. Very soon after our sleep was interrupted by a sergeant with a flashlight who yelled 'Mission' I shouted at him but he said, 'The mission is in jeopardy, you have to go back.' We dragged our 'you know what's' to briefing where we were told that 'the Germans are pushing us into the sea.' We had to go back on a tactical mission to support our troops.

'For me, this was a more difficult mission. The B-17 has a nose hatch that is above your head. When I first saw a Flying Fortress, I learned why we had to do all those chin ups in navigation school. Well, on the second mission of June 6, I couldn't make it up wearing my flying suit, Mae West, flak suit and carrying a parachute. I got to the nose by the rear door, crawling though the bomb bay.

'We left the English coast at 15,000 feet at 19:55 hours and we reached the IP at 20:15 at 20,000 feet. We did not bomb the primary target, however and after several turns, we found a 'target of opportunity' a 'railroad choke point in the southern part of Flers.'

'The mission report tells us that we bombed at 22,000 at 20:58. It was a visual bomb run at Pont L'Eveque on a heading of 160 degrees. The target is on the Touques River, about 20-25 miles east of Caen. 'Bomb' Kerns, our ball turret gunner, said that on the second bomb run, he returned his guns straight down and he could see the structure of the bridge that we bombed. He said he heard the 'clack-clack' of the anti-aircraft guns that were firing at us. He also mentioned all the gliders that were on the ground in various positions, some crashed into trees. I can confirm that we could see gliders.

'We returned to Knettishall at 23:40, which was over 25 hours later than when we first started out on June 5. Six of our aircraft landed at other fields, probably because of bad weather. When I talked to our bombardier, Charles Kemp, about the second mission he said that using a B-17 for tactical missions is a mistake, because of the great danger of hitting your own troops and pattern bombing is too wide for close engagement.

'When we finally returned to our barracks, we were allowed to sleep all day on June 7, but we had a mission on June 8 to Tours, France.'

August C. Bolino, navigator, Dan Houghton's crew, 388th Bomb Group.

'Some people gambled, some read books, some prayed. We had a Catholic priest, Father Lacey, who was quite a man. He held three services the night before we sailed, a Protestant, a Jewish and a Catholic one. I went to all three of them. He asked me what my religion was and I said, 'whatever works'; that's about the way I felt about it. [18]

'We expected it to be easier than it was. The bombers were so close together it seemed as if the whole sky was covered with bombers and we could hear them detonating on the coast and we could hear the terrible gunfire and the flashes and then the battleship *Texas* and the destroyers opened up and we thought that nobody could live through all that, so we actually thought that there wouldn't be any opposition - we'd just be able to walk straight across the beach.

'I guess no war's like you'd expect it to be. Whoever planned the whole thing didn't take into consideration that... the bombers would have made holes in the beach where you could take cover, but when the tide came in the sea would cover the holes and they would become a hazard... Our part of the landing was delayed by about thirty minutes and by that time the Germans had recovered from the artillery and the bombing and the navy

18   Lacey was subsequently awarded the DSO for his bravery on the Normandy beaches.

and the fighter bombers couldn't come any closer or we'd be at risk, so when the ramp went down on the boat, I knew we were in trouble. The first thing I heard was like a woodpecker pecking on a tree. It was bullets rattling against the ramp of the boat and then big plumes of smoke went up and I saw that Lieutenant Fitzsimmons who was a good friend of mine, his landing craft was hit by an 88 or a mortar right on the ramp and it just blew up and I thought, 'There goes one platoon.' It was terrible... But the only thing we had in mind was to take those guns... when the ramp dropped we went down and the water was ice-cold. We had these big packs on, we were carrying three days' rations - not that Rangers carry much, only D-rations, little chocolate bars and we were carrying ammunition and grenades and all these things along with a gas mask - which we never did need, fortunately. A lot of the men were wearing lifebelts and they would immediately inflate them, but I think that most of our people were smart enough not to inflate them, because if you are wearing an inflated life-jacket when the waves hit you, you turn upside down in the water and drown... and you had to get off to the right of the ramp - I'd been trained about that for years - otherwise the boat could surge forward and run over you. The water was up to my shoulders straight away and I immediately dropped my gas mask, but I reckoned that I'd rather be gassed than drown so I just made for the shore and tried to get my men together because I figured I was the only officer left and I was trying to get the men off the beach and up to the rocks where we could reform and get after those guns because that was our job.

'I saw one of my sergeants there and his left thumb was gone but he didn't look as if he was hurt too badly so I called his name and told him to get up and come with us. I rolled him over and he was dead. just in front of him was another fellow, Butch Blader, who was lying there so I hollered at him 'Let's get up and go'... and he kinda looked back over his shoulder at me and didn't say anything and when I got closer I saw that there was blood all over his back and he'd been hit in the stomach and the bullet had passed right through and come out of his spine and so I started towards the sea wall... and then I was hit by machine-gun fire in the left leg and the pain was terrible. It knocked me down and I thought, 'Well, I haven't been here ten minutes and I've already got a Purple Heart and I managed to get up and then a sniper got me in my right leg... I started out to cross the beach with thirty-five men and only six got to the top, that's all. We assumed that 'D' and 'E' and 'F' Companies had been wiped out and we hadn't heard from C company and we thought that they might have made a landing on their own and 'A' Company was just decimated, bodies were spread everywhere, you could hardly walk on the sand for bodies and I thought, 'This part of the invasion's over, I just hope that they're doing better on 'Utah' and the British beaches...'

1st Lieutenant Robert 'Bob' T. Edlin, 2nd US Rangers aboard the HMS *Prince Charles*. Later, he was officially credited as being the first American soldier to board a landing craft for the invasion.

'We left the British Channel steamer HMS *Ben Machree* for the LCA assault craft. It was a foggy, overcast morning. The seas were rough and some of the craft were swamped. Unlike many of the other landing forces not used to the heavy seas, most of us weren't bothered too much by seasickness. We carried only thermite grenades, carbines, automatic rifles and M-1s and limited food supplies with us. The only food I took along was a chocolate bar from my D-ration. Three of the companies ('F', 'D' and 'E') were assigned to go in first. If we were successful in taking the cliffs and establishing a position in the prescribed time, the other three companies ('A', 'B' and 'C') would follow up as support. First of all, we were headed toward Pointe de la Percèe on the wrong course and consequently, lost our element of surprise. The Germans saw what we were up to and lobbed shells at us as we headed west to Pointe-du-Hoc. When we finally landed, after two hours in the water, the fire was heavy. Our BAR man was the first one on the boat and he was hit by machine gun fire immediately. Most of us hustled out of the boats and managed to find some protection at the base of the cliff. Each boat had six rope ladders to fire into the rocky side of the hill. Out of half a dozen we got only one secured at the top of the cliff. 'A', 'B' and 'C' Companies and the 5th Ranger took off for the beaches in other directions, so we were all alone up there. After the hour of battle it became a mere matter of survival.'

Pfc Carl E. Bombardier, Company 'F', 2nd Ranger Battalion. He had joined the army with his hometown friend Pfc Charles H. Bellows Jr., in the tradition of the British commandos under the 'buddy' system, as volunteers in 1942. Both men were from Abington, Massachusetts. They joined the 2nd Ranger in 1943. Charlie Bellows, who was in Company 'E', reached the top of the cliffs with members of his unit. He was reported to be involved in action against one of the fortified gun positions. Bellows was later killed at Pointe-du-Hoc. Bellows Circle off Plymouth Street, Abington bears his name. Both men were 20 years old. Carl E. Bombardier was the father of nine children. He died of a heart attack in Abington, Massachusetts on 2 July 1976. One of his sons, Leon A. Bombardier, who became a captain in the US Army Corps of Engineers was named in honour of his father's squad leader, Sergeant Leon H. Otto who was also killed at Pointe-du-Hoc.

'We had a perfect landing. I didn't even get my feet wet. But when 1 looked at the beach I thought the world was coming to an end. There was no room on the beach. There was no room at the sea wall... there were just the dead.'

Ted Lapres.

'On the Normandy coast near the point where the Vire flows into the Channel is Vierville-sur-Mer. It's a tiny town of relatively no importance, except for one thing. It was here that the 2nd and 5th Ranger Battalions and the 116th Infantry Regiment made their assault landing in the invasion of Europe. We knew what Vierville looked like from the maps, aerial photos and terrain models we had studied. We had a good idea of about what we'd meet in the way of German resistance. We didn't think many of us would be alive on June 7. We knew of the obstacles in the water, the narrow strip of sand enfiladed from the bluffs above, the sea wall, the beach road, the flat open field and the high steep bluffs. We knew of the Vierville exit through the bluffs where a narrow road ran from Vierville to the coast road.

There were minefields galore. Yes, we knew what to expect, or thought we did.

'That night, standing on the deck of HMS *Prince Baudouin* I watched the Normandy coast burn. I didn't get much time to sleep, for I took three tours of Officer of the Deck. It seemed the thing to do. Captain Bill Wise, Company 'C' CO had a rough job. Major Dick Sullivan had a rough job too. I was HQ Company Commander with my company split all over the place. Chances were we wouldn't set up a decent CP for a couple of days and till then I would be just an amanuensis. The whole setup was good. On another ship was Lieutenant Colonel Rudder, who was both Ranger Group Commander and CO of the 2nd Rangers, which, under Captain Goranson was to cross the beach west of the Vierville exit and scramble up the bluffs and attack the enemy emplacements at La Pointe de la Percèe. Three more companies of the Second Battalion, 'D', 'E' and 'F' were to assault the cliffs at the Pointe-du-Hoc. If 'D', 'E' and 'F' were successful, the remaining two companies of the Second, 'A' and 'B;, plus the whole 5th would follow and advance on Isigne-sur-Vire. If they weren't successful, then we'd all go over the beach behind the 1st Battalion of the 116th Infantry. For communication with the 2nd at Pointe-du-Hoc, we had SCR-300s set up in the boat. If we had received no signal meaning success by H+30 minutes, it was over the beach instead of the cliffs.

'At 04:45 we loaded into the LCA. The captain bid us a 'Good luck Rangers and God Bless You' over the audio system. It sounds melodramatic now but we appreciated it then. We saw the *Texas* open up and fire its first salvo as we sailed by it. It was a terrific roar. Runge's boat began to ship water and dropped back. The radios didn't look like they were going to work. The men were getting jittery and H-Hour was still a half hour away. The sea was running from 4 to 6 feet. A couple of men got sick. We were all soaked to the skin. We could hear the planes overhead, the ships bombarding the coast. What with the Air Corps and the Navy, Normandy's defences would be a shambles by the time we hit the beach. And the minutes droned on. H-Hour. No word from the Second. A beach master's radio came through clearly to the effect 'Dog White is clear. Troops meeting no resistance.' No word from the Second. We shifted our course toward Dog beach. There would still be time to change our course for the cliffs if only the signal would come through. I'm not sure of this next, but I vaguely recall hearing a radio message from the Second. It was feeble and almost unintelligible. We weren't sure what it meant, but it didn't mean success. Colonel Schneider has waited as long as he could and now we'd have to really move to land on time. The beachmaster on Dog White had stopped his talk. We soon saw the reason why.

'We were still about a thousand yards out when A and B of the Second touched down. The ramps dropped and the men were slaughtered by machine gun fire. You could see them drop as they tried to get out. In desperation, they went over the sides and lay half drowning in the water hidden behind obstacles. A scattered few made it up the beach. Others began to move out of the water. Most made it now that they were dispersed. Except for a few Rangers and smashed boats there in that hell of fire, the beach looked empty. Colonel Schneider in the wave ahead of us watched the slaughter through his binoculars. I don't know what he thought, but I can imagine, when you remember that two months before, he had been Exec of the Second. He made a crucial decision as he watched. He shifted the whole two waves from Dog Green to Dog White where resistance seemed lighter and where, apparently, most of the 116th had landed by mistake. To shift 1,500 yards to the left when only a thousand yards from the beach was a problem the British did well. We didn't lose a single boat, we didn't get mixed up and as we came into touchdown we still had perfect formation.

'Schneider's wave hit first, we were minutes behind him and apparently to his right. By now the noise was deafening. An LCM or LCT was hit on our right by artillery and burst into flames. A minute or so later we were in the obstacles. LCI 91, 50 to 100 yards on our right was hit by artillery. The boat ground to a stop. The ramp dropped. Sullivan jumped out with me right behind him. The water wasn't as high as my boots. The coxswain had done well by us. Ten yards of shallow water amid the damnedest racket in the world. You could hear the bullets go screaming by. Somewhere a twenty or forty was beating out sixty rounds a minute. Rifle fire came from our right as did most of the MG fire. A DD tank let a round fly.

'There was the beach and then a runnel of water. An MG burst chewed the water as I jumped in. Then dry land again. The beach must have been about 30 yards wide at that time. I remember reaching the sea wall. It was packed with men two and three deep. You couldn't dig in because the rocks were 6 to 8 inches in diameter and piled deeply. The sea wall was made of wooden logs two to three feet high with breakwaters running back toward the sea. They prevented good lateral communication on the beach though they gave us protection from the flanking fire that poured down the beach from our right.

'I tried to get my life preservers off. They wouldn't come. I rolled over, still no luck. I couldn't go on like that so I stood up and still no luck. I looked around. It was my first look at men in combat. They were huddled in against the sea wall, cringing at every bullet. Artillery fire was churning the water's edge. To our left I saw LCI 92 touchdown. Wham! An artillery round caught the starboard ramp. Must have hit a flamethrower there; for the whole side of the ship burst into flames that spread to the deck. I looked back at our LCA, men were still coming out. There was Father Lacy, the last man coming out. He wasn't ten yards from the boat when Wham! Our engine compartment was hit by artillery. I don't know what happened to the crew. They'd done their job well - too well, for the cox'n was too hard on the beach to back off.

'By now my men were dropping around me and in the adjacent bays. I yelled to a radio man who stood up and cut my preservers off. 'Anybody hit?'

'Yea, McCullough got a slug in the back of his leg.'

'One man, my messenger, only two men behind me was hit. Not bad for thirty-three men. I called for Sullivan.

'Over here, Red.' He was in the next bay. I slipped over and made my report, one casualty and the rest of HQ dispersed in these three bays. We passed the word for Colonel Schneider. He was 50 yards to our left giving orders to the company commanders. However, I remained on the right while Sullivan went over to Schneider.

'I began checking the men, making sure they still had their weapons and ammo, getting them more collected for the next move, while wondering what it was to be. Apparently some infantrymen or Rangers had worked their way off the beach and up the hillside, for there was a fire fight to our right, up on the bluff. The terrain was different from the maps. The high steep hill was 100-150 yards in front of us, covered with smoke and flame from a grass fire to our right. The terrain was flat from the foot of the hill to the coast road in front of us with a battered little stone wall and then the wooden sea wall. Wooden sea wall! Christ! It was supposed to be stone! We were on the wrong beach! We couldn't be to the right of Vierville because there'd be cliffs in front of us and the Pointe de la Percèe on our right. Therefore, we must be to the left. The next sea wall was Dog White. I looked around more carefully. The sea wall ended three or four bays to my right. I could see farther down to the right one, perhaps two DD tanks of the 743rd backing down to the water and then slowly coming across the beach, each time giving five or six men cover to cross the beach. Back and forth, but that was 200 or 300 yards away.

'Not ten yards to me right a grizzled old Engineer Sergeant set a heavy MG tripod down in a hole in the stone breakwaters or retards. He then went back to my left. A moment later he returned with a heavy gun. A thin Engineer Lieutenant in a green sweater was carrying ammunition. Together they very calmly set up their gun in that exposed gap in the wall. The Sergeant very methodically began to traverse and search the hill to our right where the fire fight appeared to be. The lieutenant and I'll always remember the disdain he showed, turned around with his hands on hips, surveyed the men huddled at the sea wall and spat out something to the effect, 'and you men call yourselves soldiers.' He tried to organize his men. Then the 116th. But to no avail.

'By now Colonel Schneider had given the word to advance. The gap in the wire was to our left, HQ to follow one of Company 'C's MG sections. 1st Lieutenant Howard E. Van Riper, my Exec and Commo Platoon leader and I drifted to the left with the Company, leaving the Engineer lieutenant with his hands still on hips looking disgusted. (I heard he was killed a half hour or so later). We found the gap. A line Company was going through. Some Heine was firing from the right along the coast road. There was a shattered stone building, probably a pill box just across the road. Charlie Company was moving through now. I tagged on, rushed across the road. Lying stomach down on a stone slab on the left side of the pill box was little Vullo, the smallest man in the Battalion, having general repairs done on his buttocks. He hadn't crossed the road fast enough. We trotted down a little path and then the column stopped, hit the dirt. It wasn't too comfortable there in the open so I shifted my men to the left into a small gully or ditch. The column moved again, stopped, moved. There was heavy brush at the base of the hill and a flagstone path leading through. About six stone steps and then a path leading up and right. The column stopped as I reached the last step. I sat down and looked back toward the beach. Men were still coming through the gap in the wire.

'The column moved on, up the steep slope, the smoke was getting bad. After about 50 yards we were gasping for breath and gulping in smoke, our eyes were watering and we couldn't see ahead. I passed the word for gas masks. We had the new assault masks with the canister on the face piece. Mine wouldn't come out. I put my helmet between my legs. Finally got my mask on - took a deep breath and almost smothered. I had forgotten to take the covering plug out of the canister. I felt like I was smothering to death, I couldn't get the plug out. I ripped off my mask; my helmet slipped from my legs and started to roll down the hill. Sergeant Graves stopped it. Now I was choking with smoke. I finally got the mask and helmet on, took three steps and was out of the smoke. I was so furious; I kept the mask on for fifty feet more just to spite myself.

'We'd left the path now (it curved back to the left past a little shack) and continued to the top of the hill. We saw our first German, a dead one, lying in a little hollow just below the crest. We'd never seen a dead man before. He was sort of greenish yellow. We thought he was a wax booby-trapped dummy. It wasn't 'till much later that we realized that that was the first dead enemy we'd seen. In the hollow, we paused for breath before crossing a tiny stone wall into the hedgerow country. At the top of the hill we paused, looked over the scene again and then moved to the right, parallel to the beach. Charlie Company's 81 mm mortars and a light MG section were emplaced in the far western hedge row prepared to fire parallel to the beach. I dispersed HQ behind in the field behind the mortars and left a non-com in charge. Just as I left, Van Riper came up with the rest of HQ and dispersed them in the same field. There was scattered small arms fire to the west and south of us and some low velocity artillery was passing close overhead heading for the beach. Captain Bill Wise told me I'd find Major Sullivan and Colonel Schneider at the southern end of the hedgerow but not to go into the open field beyond because the enemy was to our front. I found Sully and Colonel Schneider at the gate at the end of the field. Unfortunately there was no known situation for Sullivan to give me. All he could say was that he had seen a patrol move off to the SW along the fence toward the far hedgerow. He had me move out along the fence to see if I drew fire, because that would be the best route to move the portion of the battalion that had not displaced along the crest. I zigzagged about 75 to 100 yards before I reached cover. I had drawn enough fire to mention most of it friendly anyway. There was a dead German in the hedgerow.'

Captain (later Major-General) John C. Raaen Jr., HQ Company, 5th Ranger Battalion who was awarded the Silver Star.

'The alarm sounded in the early hours of June 6. A loudspeaker blazed the words 'wakey, wakey, yavoe, yavoe'. It was time to board the assault craft and leave our British mother ship for the assault on the French coast in a quest to free Europe from the grasp of the madman, Adolph Hitler. The seas were extremely rough, waves so high that many times it seemed the assault craft was in a great hole surrounded by water. Rangers were seated on low benches on each side facing each other and men straddled a low bench in the centre facing the exit ramp, while a British officer and a seaman directed the craft from the front. This boat was an English design used for commando raids. It presented a low profile, unlike the American landing craft and produced very little wake in the water; therefore its presence was hard to detect. I was nineteen years old and was about to take part in an event that would affect the course of history, defeating those who would enslave humanity and rule the world by force. This day would change my life forever; if I lived to survive it. My youth would be sacrificed. I would be entering a world of kill or be killed. Stress and fatigue would be tested to the limit of human endurance, a trial by fire. The emotional strain of not helping a fallen comrade in order to reach and accomplish your assigned mission would take its toll. Somewhere in the catacombs of my brain the horrible memories would lay dormant to be recalled when I would lie awake in the dark of night.

'We were lowered into the wild waters of the English Channel in our landing craft assault boats. Some of the men were seasick and it was necessary to use our helmets to bail out the landing craft due to the tumultuous sea swells and the raging storm. Because of the rigorous training we had been given for this invasion of the Normandy coast, I was not frightened. We boarded the landing craft ten to twelve miles from the beach, making us vulnerable to enemy fire from the big guns on Pointe-du-Hoc. The landing area was fortified with mines and metal barriers to repel invading forces. The enemy had many fortifications and concealed underground connecting tunnels. Artillery and machine gun emplacements were strategically placed to kill men as they left their boats. German guns were also being fired parallel to the beach to achieve the maximum kill. Our navy and air force were bombing the beach creating smoke that concealed our landing area from us, causing much confusion. Casualties were heavy; American self-reliance came into play. Plans were scrapped and on-the-spot decisions were made by individuals who saved the day.

'The command came to drop the ramp. I jumped into the water, which was knee deep and coloured red by blood. The bullets, mortar and artillery fire were intense. The German 88 artillery gun was a deadly and accurate weapon that sank many craft and killed a great number of our men. The enemy targeted the ramp openings on the landing craft, killing men before they could get off the boat. It was a slaughter. Men were dying all around me. Explosives were going off on the beach ahead of us; enormous sheets of fire from artillery guns, rifle and mortar fire blanketed the beach. Machine gun bullets were dimpled the water like rain. Our immediate objective was to get off the beach alive. I was a Bangalore torpedo man. My job was to precede the troops and blow up the land mines and barbed wire so that the soldiers could advance. Once I set the fuse I would dive in the opposite direction. The subsequent explosion would lift me into the air and I would land on the ground in a dazed condition. I didn't stay dazed long as my life and the lives of my fellow Rangers depended on getting off the beach.

'We fought our way up the hill to the cover of some hedgerows that were practically impossible to penetrate. Looking down at the incoming forces presented a horrible sight of men being blown to pieces. I lost my religion. Crawling though the hedgerows was torturous, so I threw away all my gear except my gun and ammunition. We were forced to kill many Germans and in turn many of my comrades were killed or wounded. War is hell.

'Our group made the greatest penetration into enemy territory on D-Day; twenty-three of us were officially listed as missing in action. At one point we were ambushed on a road between two hedgerows. The Germans were throwing hand grenades at us from behind the bushes. Rangers grabbed the grenades before they went off and threw them back before they could explode on our side of the bushes. Their own weapons killed them.

'Our assignment was to reach Pointe-du-Hoc and destroy the big guns that could annihilate our invasion forces. It had to be done and we were expendable. These huge 155 mm cannon could cover both 'Omaha' and 'Utah' beaches and the incoming landing force and were capable of destroying ships ten or twelve miles out to sea.

'At the rendezvous point near a French farmhouse we were shocked to find that we only had 23 men, having started at the beach with 72 men in Company 'A'. The combined forces should have equalled 560 men. We had a problem. The question was 'were we the only ones that got off the beach, did the invasion fail?' There was no time to ponder. Our mission was to destroy the big guns at the point so we took off at a run.

'The dirt country roads were lined with hedgerows making them seem like tunnels affording cover for the enemy to trap us so we took to the open countryside. There were many fire fights and in the process we captured about twenty prisoners. Our fighting force practically equalled the number of captives. What should we do; take them with us, kill them or turn them lose? We disarmed them and chose the latter. We ran like hell, fighting and dodging battles until we heard that sweet sound of an English-speaking voice that demanded the password. We had arrived at Pointe-du-Hoc and joined the 2nd Ranger band. To our dismay we learned that the big guns were not in place on the cliffs but had been moved elsewhere. Telephone poles were put in their place in the pillbox to deceive the allied reconnaissance. Fortunately, members of the 2nd Ranger band found the hiding place of the big guns and destroyed their firing mechanisms. Hurray!

'Our men were deployed with the 2nd band to secure the point and block the German advance. Night fell and the enemy attacked with vengeance and enormous firepower, shouting and blowing whistles. At one point they were within fifty yards of us. To our men in the foxholes it was practically hand to hand combat; we were in a survival mode. Food or water had not passed our lips in days. Our ammunition supplies were very low. On D+1 our combined forces of the 5th and 2nd Ranger battalions consisted of only 90 men able to bear arms. We held out.

'The situation was becoming desperate. We were running out of food, water and just about everything plus the batteries were dead in our radios. Seven of us, led by Captain Parker, volunteered to try to make contact with the main force on the beach. The patrol advanced, only to discover we were in the middle of a land mine field in open ground with 20 yards to go before we could reach the shelter of a small mound on the cliff edge. German machine gun fire opened up on us before we could reach the berm, killing one man; my best friend. While trying to make the run for shelter I was shot. My comrades pulled me into a crevice in the cliff but had to leave me to continue on with their mission. I realized that my chance of coming out of this alive was practically nil. The primeval will to live kicked in. The cheek of my left buttock was blown open; it looked like a big red bowl of Jell-O.

The army provided us with two first aid kits to use in the event of being wounded. Sulpha drugs were included. I spread all of the drugs on the one wound and applied the bandage. After taking off my canteen belt I found another wound where a bullet had entered my back. An unknown force told me to exchange the first bandage with the drugs on it and apply it to the newly discovered wound. I put the new bandage on my buttocks thereby having the sulpha drug on both wounds. I also spit on the wounds for some reason. A decision had to be made. 'Do I stay here and hope they come back for me?' Not very likely. I chose to start crawling back towards the point. Sometimes I would try standing part way up until I could not stand the pain then I would drop to my knees and crawl. At one point a bullet went by my ear. The nearest shell hole was my refuge. I put my helmet on the end of my rifle and raised it, hoping to draw fire - no shot. A sniper was in the tree and waved for me to surrender. I started towards him half-walking, half-crawling but decided I would rather be dead than a prisoner, so dove into the bushes. The expected bullet never came; he let me get away. Not all Germans are bad guys.

'Somehow I kept going and eventually came to an open field. I did not hear or see anyone or anything. A sixth sense told me to turn and fire my weapon. I killed a German lying in wait for me. He had fired his rifle but missed his mark. By this time I was pretty well out of my head having had no food or water and having lost lots of blood. The German foxhole looked like a pretty safe place to be so I crawled in. I lay next to the dead German, ate his black bread and promptly threw up. I then started to hallucinate, seeing Mickey Mouse and Goofy on a large screen in full colour. I decided to wait four hours and then kill myself, as I did not relish a slow death. Luck was on my side; a US patrol picked me up.

'I had cheated the grim reaper. The clothes on my left side were coated with dried blood, I was filthy and hadn't eaten, shaved or bathed since the landing. In my delirious state I insisted on rejoining A company. The medics picked me up and carried me to a landing craft to evacuate me. My recollection of the hospital ship was a scene of blood with maimed and dying men everywhere.

'I was alive.'

'*The Day I lost My Religion.* Private James W. Gabaree, Company 'A', 5th Ranger Battalion.

'We were about 200 feet from the beach when a shell blew off the front of our landing craft, destroying the ramp. My two best buddies were right in front of me and they were both killed. When we went over the side of the landing craft (to avoid machine gun fire), the water was about 12 feet deep. After the shell hit, it was pretty much everyone for themselves. I was holding a .45 pistol and carrying a bazooka with eight shells; it was so heavy that I just went right under the water, so I had to let everything go except the shells. Eventually when I got to the beach I picked up a German rifle that I used. When we all got together on the beach, things were getting kind of bad. Fortunately, Colonel Schneider called the battleship *Texas* for support fire and it made a direct hit on the German pillbox. Two destroyers [USS *Satterlee* and HMS *Talybont*] took turns all day long firing at targets. They saved us; they were terrific. When we were on the beach, there were two other Rangers and myself running and a German machine gun was firing at us. We hid behind an anti-tank obstacle. The three of us ducked behind it. We then headed towards the front again, towards the street. It was terrible; there were bodies all over the place. They wiped out almost the entire 116th Infantry Regiment; they just murdered them. They were floating all over the place, there was blood in the water - it was just dark.

Ray Alm, Company 'B', US 2nd Ranger Battalion.

'We were late in getting to the beaches. Our rope ladders got wet on the way over. We were dumped out and had to wade several hundred feet in to the beach and all the time the Germans were firing at us from the top of the big bluff we had to storm. Some of us were shot crossing the sand to the foot of the cliff. When we climbed, the Germans shot down at us. Finally, we threw grenades at the cliff, making furrows up the side and giving us some protection.

'Then we all went up and chased those Germans, killing a lot of them. They had left a little dog up there in a shack. He would respond to English, but he would stand up when you talked to him in German... But that dog turned out to be a fifth columnist. He licked the wounded and annoyed them until we had to slit his throat.

'I saw a German officer shoot one of his men in the back when he started to walk over to us with his hands up. One of our guys saw a flag of surrender and stood up to wave to the Germans to come on over and was shot between the eyes.'

Ranger Alban Meccia's account in *The Saturday Evening Post*.

'We landed and fired off our rockets. The ramp goes down and... I stepped off into water over my head. The guys pulled me out and we just rushed to the base of that cliff and grabbed any rope we could get and up the cliff we went just as fast as we could go. The wound wasn't bad; it had gone through the muscle on my right side.

'Captain Baugh of Company 'E' was the first person I ran across on top. He had been shot and had his hand practically blown off and wasn't in such good shape. We kept right on going saying, 'Captain, we'll send you back a medic.' My platoon couldn't wait for nothing. We had our assignment and we in Company 'D' depended on a lot of speed. My second platoon went ahead in a rush. We had some confrontations coming out of shell craters. As we were charging out of a shell crater, a machine gun opened up and Morris Webb, one of my sergeants, jumped back into the crater right on top of one of his men's bayonet that went right through his side.

'We didn't stop; we played it just like a football game, charging hard and low. We went into the shell craters for protection because there were snipers around and machine guns firing at us. We'd wait for a moment and if the fire lifted we were out of that crater and into the next one. We ran as fast as we could over to the gun positions - to the one that we were assigned to. There were no guns in the positions!

'There was an anti-aircraft position off to our right several hundred yards and a machine gun off to the left. There was another machine gun that we had gotten on our way in. The antiaircraft gun was firing flat trajectory at us and by the time we got to the road I only had about a dozen men left. We were up on top of the cliffs around 1930.

'The road was our next objective. We were supposed to get into the coastal road and set up a roadblock, which we did. We were the first ones at the coastal road. We were in the midst of doing this when all of a sudden we heard noise and clanking. We laid low in our ditch on the side of the road. It was an armed combat patrol of Germans loaded with heavy equipment, mortars and machine guns headed in the other direction toward 'Utah'. I'd got ten or twelve guys and I was about to take on fifty or sixty when we've still got our mission to accomplish, so we let them go. Sergeant Koenig destroyed the communications along the coastal road by blowing up the telephone poles. Then Jack Kuhn (my platoon sergeant while I was the acting platoon leader) and I went down this sunken road not knowing where the hell it was going, but it was going inland. We came upon this vale or little draw with camouflage all over it. Lo and behold, we peeked over this hedgerow and there were the guns. [Five of the six guns were well camouflaged but unguarded in an orchard 2½ miles further inland. One had been damaged by bombing and had been removed it for repair]. It was pure luck. They were all sitting in proper firing condition, with ammunition piled up neatly; everything at the ready. But they were pointed at 'Utah' Beach, not 'Omaha'. There was nobody at the emplacement. We looked around cautiously and over about a hundred yards away in a corner of a field was a vehicle with what looked like an officer talking to his men. We decided let's take a chance. I said, 'Jack, you cover me and I'm going in there and destroy them.' All I had was two thermite grenades - his and mine. I went in and put the thermite grenades in the traversing mechanism and that knocked out two of them because that melted their gears in a moment. Then I broke their sights. We ran back to the road, which was a hundred or so yards back and got all the other thermites from the remainder of my guys manning the roadblock and rushed back and put the grenades in traversing mechanisms, elevation mechanisms and banged the sights. There was no noise to that. There is no noise to a thermite, so no one saw us. Jack said, 'Hurry up and get out of there, Len.' I came up over the hedgerow with him and suddenly the whole place blew up. We thought it was a short round from the Texas but it was another patrol from Company 'E', led by Sergeant Rupinski, around to the left of us. They came upon the ammo depot and blew it up. We went flying. Dust and everything was settling on us and we got up and ran like two scared rabbits as fast as we could back to our men at the roadblock.

'We had the guns out of action before 0830 and Sergeant Harry Tate volunteered to go back to Colonel Rudder and report the mission was accomplished and that we had the roadblock set up; and Sergeant Gordon Luning volunteered to take the message via a different route.

'Those guns had not been recently moved to that position. They'd been there a long time. There wasn't one bomb crater near them. They were so well camouflaged that the air force and whoever did the bombings of them never saw them and their photos never saw them. The rest of the Pointe was perforated. They'd been blowing the hell out of that for four months. No wonder they'd moved those guns. You couldn't find a straight piece of land to do anything on at the Pointe.'

Sergeant Leonard Lomell, who received the Distinguished Service Cross. To this point, the 2nd Ranger's casualties were probably 30-40 but later that day the German 1st Battalion, 914th Regiment began a series of counter-attacks that nearly wiped out the small bridgehead and caused most casualties. That night the 2nd Rangers were driven into a small enclave along the cliff, barely 200 yards wide, but the they held out until noon on 8 June, helped by fire from destroyers, when they were relieved by Lieutenant Colonel Schneider's men. By then 2nd Ranger casualties were 135 killed, wounded and missing - a casualty rate of 60 per cent. Company 'C', 2nd Ranger Battalion suffered 50 per cent casualties (38 out of 64 men) clearing the German positions at Pointe de la Percée before proceeding overland to Pointe-du-Hoc.

On the morning of 8 June the 116th Infantry Regiment of the 29th Infantry Division moved out of Vierville towards Ste-Pierre-du-Mont. The 5th Ranger Infantry Battalion which was attached to the 116th led the column. Also in that column were the 743rd Tank Battalion and several divisional units. When the 5th Rangers arrived at my CP in Ste-Pierre-du-Mont at 0845, Colonel Schneider took over the plans and operations of the two 5th Ranger Companies and the Provisional Company of the 2nd Rangers that I had with me in Ste-Pierre. There was even a part of a platoon from Company 'F' with us under Lieutenant Reville. He had run a patrol from the Pointe to Ste-Pierre-du-Mont during the night on 8th and 9th June. The attack on

Pointe-du-Hoc was almost routine. At 0900, the battalion attacked toward the northwest, with 'C', 'D' and 'F' Companies, a platoon of Company 'A' and the Provisional Company of the 2nd Rangers. The action was all over by 1000 hours with the three companies of the 2nd Ranger Infantry Battalion relieved after their two days of dreadful fighting, isolated and badly outnumbered. Meanwhile Companies 'B' and 'E' of the 5th Rangers led the 116th Infantry Regiments and the tanks of the 743rd down the coastal road towards Grandcamp-les-Bains. One Infantry Battalion and some of the tanks peeled off from the column and attacked the Pointe from the southwest. Unfortunately, this attack ended up as a blue on blue action with the tanks and infantry firing on the just rescued 2nd Ranger positions. One report gives two Rangers' KIA and six WIA during that skirmish. The mission of 'B' and 'E' Companies of the 5th Rangers was to take and hold the high ground west of the sluice gate at Grandcamp-les-Bains. At 1000 with Company 'B' leading, the force moved into the outskirts of Grandcamp-les-Bains. Initially, no fire was received, but as they reached the bridge leading into the town, they received heavy mortar and machine gun fire. The two companies withdrew to the high ground east of town where they were reinforced by Company 'D' which had just come from Pointe-du-Hoc. The 2nd and 3rd Battalions of the 116th Infantry passed through the three Ranger Companies and with the support of the tanks, artillery and naval gunfire captured the town. Companies 'A', 'C' and 'F' proceeded from Pointe-du-Hoc to the southern edges of Grandcamp-les-Bains under Major Sullivan. My headquarters element was given the mission of clearing the houses along the road of any German stragglers. I set up four teams of four Rangers, two for the right side of the road and two for the left. I led the first team on the left. The team would enter a house. If the door were locked, stick a bayonet in the keyhole, fire one round and kick open the door. It works! First man up the stairs to clean out the second floor. The second man was his backup. Third and fourth manhandle the main floor. Then the first two finished take the basement. The teams would leapfrog from house to house. Back in the countryside, we worked our way towards Maisy, halting about a mile and a half to the northeast where we snuggled into the ditches and hedgerows for the night.

Index

Index